W<small>THE</small>EST INDIAN
AMERICANS

Senior Consulting Editor

Senator Daniel Patrick Moynihan

Consulting Editors

Ann Orlov
Managing Editor, Harvard
Encyclopedia of American
Ethnic Groups

M. Mark Stolarik
*President, The Balch Institute
for Ethnic Studies, Philadelphia*

David M. Reimers
*Professor of History,
New York University*

James F. Watts
*Chairman, History Department,
City College of New York*

W^{THE}EST INDIAN
AMERICANS

Miriam Klevan

CHELSEA HOUSE PUBLISHERS
New York   Philadelphia

On the cover: West Indian American children sit on a front porch on Blue Hills Ave. in Boston.

Chelsea House Publishers
Editor-in-Chief: Nancy Toff
Executive Editor: Remmel T. Nunn
Managing Editor: Karyn Gullen Browne
Copy Chief: Juliann Barbato
Picture Editor: Adrian G. Allen
Art Director: Maria Epes
Manufacturing Manager: Gerald Levine

The Peoples of North America
Senior Editor: Sean Dolan

Staff for THE WEST INDIAN AMERICANS
Assistant Editor: Elise Donner
Copy Editor: Michael Goodman
Editorial Assistant: Gregory R. Rodríguez
Picture Research: PAR/NYC
Assistant Art Director: Loraine Machlin
Senior Designer: Noreen M. Lamb
Production Manager: Joseph Romano
Production Coordinator: Marie Claire Cebrián
Cover Illustration: Paul Biniasz
Banner Design: Hrana L. Janto

First Printing

1 3 5 7 9 8 6 4 2

Library of Congress Cataloging-in-Publication Data
Klevan, Miriam.
  The West Indian Americans.

  (The Peoples of North America)
  Bibliography: p.
  Includes index.
  Summary: Discusses the history, culture, and religion of the West Indians, factors encouraging their emigration, and their acceptance as an ethnic group in North America.
  1. West Indian Americans—History—Juvenile literature.   2. West Indian Americans—Social life and customs—Juvenile literature.   3. West Indian Americans—Cultural assimilation—Juvenile literature. [1. West Indian Americans]
I. Title.   II. Series.

Library of Congress Cataloging-in-Publication Data

E184.W54K57   1988   970.004'969729   87-36825
ISBN 1-55546-140-9
     0-7910-0308-6 (pbk.)

CONTENTS

THE PEOPLES OF NORTH AMERICA

CHELSEA HOUSE PUBLISHERS

A NATION
OF NATIONS

Daniel Patrick Moynihan

The Constitution of the United States begins: "We the People of the United States . . ." Yet, as we know, the United States is not made up of a single group of people. It is made up of many peoples. Immigrants from Europe, Asia, Africa, and Central and South America settled in North America seeking a new life filled with opportunities unavailable in their homeland. Coming from many nations, they forged one nation and made it their own. More than 100 years ago, Walt Whitman expressed this perception of America as a melting pot: "Here is not merely a nation, but a teeming Nation of nations."

Although the ingenuity and acts of courage of these immigrants, our ancestors, shaped the North American way of life, we sometimes take their contributions for granted. This fine series, *The Peoples of North America*, examines the experiences and contributions of the immigrants and how these contributions determined the future of the United States and Canada.

Immigrants did not abandon their ethnic traditions when they reached the shores of North America. Each ethnic group had its own customs and traditions, and each brought different experiences, accomplishments, skills, values, styles of dress, and tastes in food that lingered long after its arrival. Yet this profusion of differences created a singularity, or bond, among the immigrants.

The United States and Canada are unusual in this respect. Whereas religious and ethnic differences have sparked intolerance throughout the rest of the world—from the 17th-century religious wars to the 19th-century nationalist movements in Europe to the near extermination of the Jewish people under Nazi Germany—North Americans have struggled to learn how to respect each other's differences and live in harmony.

Millions of immigrants from scores of homelands brought diversity to our continent. In a mass migration, some 12 million immigrants passed through the waiting rooms of New York's Ellis Island; thousands more came to the West Coast. At first, these immigrants were welcomed because labor was needed to meet the demands of the Industrial Age. Soon, however, the new immigrants faced the prejudice of earlier immigrants who saw them as a burden on the economy. Legislation was passed to limit immigration. The Chinese Exclusion Act of 1882 was among the first laws closing the doors to the promise of America. The Japanese were also effectively excluded by this law. In 1924, Congress set immigration quotas on a country-by-country basis.

Such prejudices might have triggered war, as they did in Europe, but North Americans chose negotiation and compromise instead. This determination to resolve differences peacefully has been the hallmark of the peoples of North America.

The remarkable ability of Americans to live together as one people was seriously threatened by the issue of slavery. It was a symptom of growing intolerance in the world. Thousands of settlers from the British Isles had arrived in the colonies as indentured servants, agreeing to work for a specified number of years on farms or as apprentices in return for passage to America and room and board. When the first Africans arrived in the then-British colonies during the 17th century, some colonists thought that they too should be treated as indentured servants. Eventually, the question of whether the Africans should be viewed as indentured, like the English, or as slaves who could be owned for life, was considered in a Maryland court. The court's calamitous decree held that blacks were slaves bound to lifelong servitude, and so were their children. America went through a time of moral examination and civil war before it finally freed African slaves and their descendants. The principle that all people are created equal had faced its greatest challenge and survived.

Yet the court ruling that set blacks apart from other races fanned flames of discrimination that burned long after slavery was abolished—and that still flicker today. The concept of racism had existed for centuries in countries throughout the world. For instance, when the Manchus conquered China in the 13th century, they decreed that Chinese and Manchus could not intermarry. To impress their superiority on the conquered Chinese, the Manchus ordered all Chinese men to wear their hair in a long braid called a queue.

By the 19th century, some intellectuals took up the banner of racism, citing Charles Darwin. Darwin's scientific studies hypothesized that highly evolved animals were dominant over other animals. Some advocates of this theory applied it to humans, asserting that certain races were more highly evolved than others and thus were superior.

This philosophy served as the basis for a new form of discrimination, not only against nonwhite people but also against various ethnic groups. Asians faced harsh discrimination and were depicted by popular 19th-century newspaper cartoonists as depraved, degenerate, and deficient in intelligence. When the Irish flooded American cities to escape the famine in Ireland, the cartoonists caricatured the typical "Paddy" (a common term for Irish immigrants) as an apelike creature with jutting jaw and sloping forehead.

By the 20th century, racism and ethnic prejudice had given rise to virulent theories of a Northern European master race. When Adolf Hitler came to power in Germany in 1933, he popularized the notion of Aryan supremacy. *Aryan*, a term referring to the Indo-European races, was applied to so-called superior physical characteristics such as blond hair, blue eyes, and delicate facial features. Anyone with darker and heavier features was considered inferior. Buttressed by these theories, the German Nazi state from

1933 to 1945 set out to destroy European Jews, along with Poles, Russians, and other groups considered inferior. It nearly succeeded. Millions of these people were exterminated.

The tragedies brought on by ethnic and racial intolerance throughout the world demonstrate the importance of North America's efforts to create a society free of prejudice and inequality.

A relatively recent example of the New World's desire to resolve ethnic friction nonviolently is the solution the Canadians found to a conflict between two ethnic groups. A long-standing dispute as to whether Canadian culture was properly English or French resurfaced in the mid-1960s, dividing the peoples of the French-speaking Quebec Province from those of the English-speaking provinces. Relations grew tense, then bitter, then violent. The Royal Commission on Bilingualism and Biculturalism was established to study the growing crisis and to propose measures to ease the tensions. As a result of the commission's recommendations, all official documents and statements from the national government's capital at Ottawa are now issued in both French and English, and bilingual education is encouraged.

The year 1980 marked a coming of age for the United States's ethnic heritage. For the first time, the U.S. Census asked people about their ethnic background. Americans chose from more than 100 groups, including French Basque, Spanish Basque, French Canadian, Afro-American, Peruvian, Armenian, Chinese, and Japanese. The ethnic group with the largest response was English (49.6 million). More than 100 million Americans claimed ancestors from the British Isles, which includes England, Ireland, Wales, and Scotland. There were almost as many Germans (49.2 million) as English. The Irish-American population (40.2 million) was third, but the next largest ethnic group, the Afro-Americans, was a distant fourth (21 million). There was a sizable group of French ancestry (13 million), as well as of Italian (12 million). Poles, Dutch, Swedes, Norwegians, and Russians followed. These groups, and other smaller ones, represent the wondrous profusion of ethnic influences in North America.

Canada, too, has learned more about the diversity of its population. Studies conducted during the French/English conflict showed that Canadians were descended from Ukrainians, Germans, Italians, Chinese, Japanese, native Indians, and Eskimos, among others. Canada found it had no ethnic majority, although nearly half of its immigrant population had come from the British Isles. Canada, like the United States, is a land of immigrants for whom mutual tolerance is a matter of reason as well as principle.

The people of North America are the descendants of one of the greatest migrations in history. And that migration is not over. Koreans, Vietnamese, Nicaraguans, Cubans, and many others are heading for the shores of North America in large numbers. This mix of cultures shapes every aspect of our lives. To understand ourselves, we must know something about our diverse ethnic ancestry. Nothing so defines the North American nations as the motto on the Great Seal of the United States: *E Pluribus Unum*— Out of Many, One.

A PROUD COMMUNITY

The British West Indies are a scattered group of former British dependencies and current members of the British Commonwealth of Nations. Located primarily in the Caribbean, these islands include Jamaica, the Bahamas, Bermuda, the Leeward Islands (St. Kitts, Nevis, Antigua, Montserrat, and the British Virgin Islands), the Windward Islands (St. Vincent, St. Lucia, Dominica, and Grenada), Barbados, Trinidad and Tobago, as well as Belize (formerly British Honduras) in Central America, and Guyana (formerly British Guiana) in South America. Eighty percent of the entire British West Indian population is black and mulatto (people with both white and black ancestors); Jamaica is home to about one-half of this population.

Double Outsiders

Today, more than 3 million natives of the West Indies and the Caribbean make their home in the United States. In fact, British West Indians constitute the largest black population to migrate voluntarily to America. By 1970, there were 78,000 West Indian–born blacks living in the United States and 52,000 second-generation residents. In 1972, the total British West Indian population in America was placed at 315,000, with 222,000 residing in New York and New Jersey. Approximately 60 percent of the British West Indian population in the United States is of the third or later generation, with many of them descendants of the first great wave of immigration. Most live in cities on the East or West Coast.

Most British West Indian immigrants came to North America in one of two great waves. The first took place in the early decades of the 20th century; the second began in approximately 1969 and has continued to the present. These black and mulatto West Indian immigrants have occupied a peculiar place in North American society. Despite their ability to speak the language of their adopted country, an advantage most immigrant groups have not shared, and their generally high rate of literacy, West Indian immigrants have had to face racial discrimination as well as the problem of balancing and resolving a complex sense of national identity. All too often, West Indians in America have found themselves to be "double" outsiders, excluded from white society because they are black and from black society because they are West Indian. Although racism does exist in the British West Indies, with mulattoes traditionally accorded greater status than blacks, the class system has allowed for the development of a respected middle class composed of both mulattoes and blacks. In North American society, the West Indian immigrant has faced a more pervasive and restrictive racism than that he knew at home. In spite of this, West Indians have consistently fared well in North America. Although they have never accounted for more than one percent of the black population in the United States, they have contributed disproportionately to the black community's business and professional class and have provided the United States with many of its black leaders. The history of the black struggle for racial equality in America owes much to West Indians and to people of West Indian descent.

Before even the first great wave of immigration, British West Indians, both white and black, had made

significant contributions to American society. During his tempestuous 49 years, Alexander Hamilton was one of the ablest lawyers in the 13 colonies, the most trusted aide to Commander in Chief George Washington of the Continental Army, an eloquent advocate of national unity, and the first U.S. secretary of the Treasury. Hamilton was born in 1755 on Nevis, a small island in the Caribbean, to a French Huguenot mother and a Scottish father. John Brown Russwurm, a Jamaican, was the first black to graduate from an American college (Bowdoin, in 1826) and the first black to publish a newspaper in the United States, called *Freedom's Journal* (coedited with Samuel Cornish). Another little-known West Indian in early American history is Robert Brown Elliot. Born in Kingston, Jamaica, in

1842, as a young child Elliot came to the United States, where he became a printer and served in the Union navy during the Civil War. At war's end he settled in Charleston, South Carolina, and became active in Reconstruction politics. After intensive study of the law, he was admitted to the South Carolina bar in 1868. Eight years later, Elliot was elected attorney general of the state of South Carolina.

Elliot was elected twice to Congress, where he earned a reputation for eloquence. During a debate in the House of Representatives over a civil rights bill, he was verbally attacked by a fellow congressman who

Robert B. Elliot of South Carolina delivered his famous speech on civil rights in the House of Representatives on January 6, 1874. Elliot served two terms in Congress.

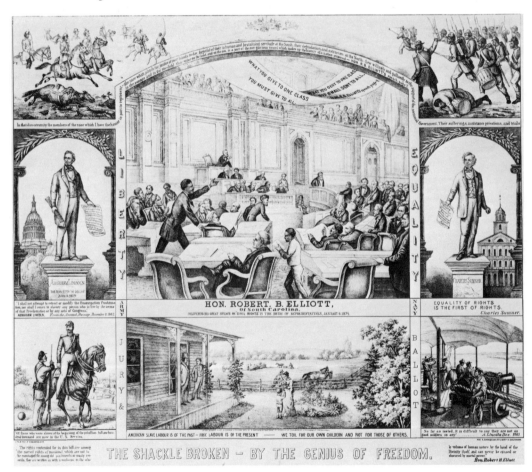

refused to address himself to a black man. Elliot responded:

> Let Harris feel that a Negro was not only too magnanimous to smite him in his weakness, but was even charitable enough to grant him the mercy of silence. . . . Assuring the gentleman that the Negro in this country aims at a Higher degree of intellect than that exhibited by him in this debate, I cheerfully commend him to the commiseration of all intelligent men the world over—black men as well as white.

Robert Brown Elliot was the first of many West Indians to fight for the rights of black people in America. In the 1920s there would be the Jamaican-born Marcus Garvey, the great black nationalist; James Weldon Johnson, a second-generation West Indian and leader of the Harlem Renaissance; and Claude McKay, a Jamaican poet best known for his writings about Harlem. Roy Innis, born in St. Croix, and Stokely Carmichael, an immigrant from Trinidad, both became leaders of the civil rights movement in the 1960s. Shirley Chisholm, who spent much of her childhood in Barbados, was the first black congresswoman in the United States, and Bahamian Sidney Poitier became an actor known for roles that helped to break black stereotypes in the entertainment industry. Even today, in the collective voice of flourishing West Indian urban communities, the message of pride, self-reliance, and equality can be heard.

This late-15th-century drawing shows Columbus's fleet off Margarita Island in the Caribbean.

SUBJUGATION AND FREEDOM

In the 15th century, Christopher Columbus, a Genoese mariner sailing for Queen Isabella and King Ferdinand of Spain, happened upon the islands of the West Indies, lands then inhabited by Carib and Arawak Indians. His discovery opened the way in the 16th century for a wave of Spanish, French, and Dutch settlers. In the 17th century, the British settled in Barbados, St. Christopher, Nevis, Antigua, and Montserrat. In 1655, the British captured Jamaica from the Spanish.

Around 1640, Dutch and Portuguese traders taught British colonists in Barbados to plant and process sugarcane. It was not long before the island began to show a profit, and within 30 years, sugar was being cultivated on the other islands, and the West Indies quickly acquired a reputation in Great Britain as a place where one could get rich quick. Indeed, the West Indies soon proved themselves to be far more profitable holdings for the British than their colonies in North America.

The Means of Production

It did not take the British long to decide that a compliant labor force was necessary in order to extract the maximum profit from the islands, which led to the establishment of a system of large-scale slavery. Need-

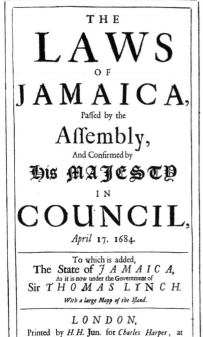

A copy of the laws of the island of Jamaica, published in London in 1684. Colonies in the West Indies were largely self-governing, and planters reacted unfavorably to attempts by the British government to regulate their extravagant way of life.

ing laborers, and having found the native population unsatisfactory (most of the Indians were exterminated by the islands' conquerors, some refused to work, some committed suicide, and others died from exhaustion and disease), the British turned to the African slave trade. In what became known as the triangular trade, Portuguese, Dutch, and British traders brought slaves from the coast of Africa to the West Indies, where some of the Africans were sold to West Indian planters. Thought too violent and savage, having come straight from the wilds of Africa, those slaves intended for sale in the American colonies also spent some time in the West Indies being "seasoned" before embarking on the last leg of their tragic journey. Before departing, the ships' captains added sugar and molasses (made by distilling the sugarcane) to their human cargo for sale to Britain's North American colonies. At Boston and other North American ports, the molasses was distilled into rum, and the ships' holds were filled with timber, fish, and furs for the return journey to England. This trade route, and the forced immigration of Africans to the West Indies and then to America, was to continue into the 1800s.

Although slavery in the West Indies was adopted primarily to maximize sugar production, the British had been importing slaves to clear the land and to work their farms since the colonies' earliest days. Colonists were already bringing African slaves with them to Barbados by 1627; by 1660, several years after the beginning of sugar production, there were 20,000 blacks on the island. During the 17th and 18th centuries, the most important British islands—Jamaica, Barbados, and the four Leeward Islands—received a total of approximately 1,480,000 slaves from the Windward Coast (modern Liberia), the Gold Coast (Ghana), and the Slave Coast (Togoland, Dahomey, and western Nigeria) of Africa.

By midcentury the black population in Barbados was greater than the white population; blacks outnumbered whites in Jamaica soon after 1670 and constituted a majority in the Leeward Islands shortly after 1680. By 1713, there were four blacks for every white

Negroes for Sale.

A Cargo of very fine stout Men and Women, in good order and fit for immediate service, just imported from the Windward Coast of Africa, in the Ship Two Brothers.— Conditions are one half Cash or Produce, the other half payable the first of January next, giving Bond and Security if required.

The Sale to be opened at 10 o'Clock each Day, in Mr. Bourdeaux's *Yard,* at No. 48, on the Bay.

May 19, 1784.　　JOHN MITCHELL.

Thirty Seasoned Negroes

To be Sold for Credit, at Private Sale.

AMONGST which is a Carpenter, none of whom are known to be dishonest.

Also, to be sold for Cash, a regular bred young Negroe Man-Cook, born in this Country, who served several Years under an exceeding good French Cook abroad, and his Wife a middle aged Washer-Woman, (both very honest) and their two Children. *Likewise,* a young Man a Carpenter.

For Terms apply to the Printer.

Eighteenth-century announcements of slave auctions, describing not only the men and women to be sold but also the terms of the sale. Slavery was the foundation on which the economy of the West Indies was built.

in the British West Indies. Whites at all levels of island society owned at least one or two black slaves and employed a white servant or two. In Barbados in 1680, for example, 19 colonists owned 200 slaves apiece, 89 colonists owned about 100 slaves each, and the remaining 65 or so colonists farmed with 3 or 4 slaves each.

British colonial society in the West Indies was one of clear class and race distinctions, ranging from the wealthy white male planter to the lowly black female field laborer. Small craftsmen lived modestly, though comfortably, in cottagelike houses, while prosperous merchants could afford a billiard room for recreation. Peasant farmers made due with a few essential pieces of furniture, while successful planters often kept both

A 19th-century watercolor sketch from the journal of Lieutenant Meynell, a British soldier, depicts the awful conditions under which slaves were transported to the West Indies.

a town and a country dwelling. Many of these larger homes, built in traditional English architectural style, proved ill suited to the climate and quickly rotted or were torn apart by tropical storms. Nevertheless, English colonists kept up Old World appearances while their black slaves lived in rows of tiny thatched huts. White servants often slung hammocks in their master's kitchen.

In spite of their attempt to transplant British society to the West Indies, the planters' conduct often deviated from what was socially acceptable in their native land. These wealthy colonists earned a reputation in Great Britain for dissipation, brutality, and heavy drinking. As late as 1810, British visitors or newly appointed governors were commenting on the colonists' loose morals, poor taste in literature, and ruthless avarice. Tacitly condoned brutality was commonplace. In 1810, Edward Huggins of the island of Nevis was acquitted of severely flogging several of his slaves in public. Five British magistrates had looked on, and none had made an attempt to stop him. Huggins then successfully sued the printer of the *St. Christopher Gazette*, who had written about the assault, for libel.

Not all colonists were content with life in the West Indies. A significant number of the planters longed to return to Britain, and by the early 19th century, a system of absentee landlordship was firmly established. Those planters who remained in the West Indies often sent their sons to Britain for an education or to America to seek their fortune. White Barbadian immigrants played a major role in shaping colonial South Carolina, where they constituted about half of the colonists who settled there between 1670 and 1680. These men became some of the most powerful in the colony. Between 1669 and 1737, 11 of the 23 governors of South Carolina were either West Indian or the sons of West Indians, and 7 of them were Barbadian. These early West Indian immigrants to South Carolina helped to develop, based on the model of the islands, the South's system of plantations and slave labor.

Slaves and Freemen

To maintain control over the large slave population, the British developed a work and disciplinary system designed to intimidate the slave population and keep it docile. In British West Indian slave law, first formulated in Barbados in the 17th century, slaves were considered chattel. Rebellion against the white masters was tried by court-martial, and even lesser offenses merited maiming, flogging, and death. By all historical accounts, slavery in the West Indies was physically much more brutal than its counterpart in the American colonies.

Woodes Rogers, appointed governor of the Bahamas in 1729, and his family wait for tea in this painting by William Hogarth. Their clothing is completely inappropriate for life in the West Indies, but the planters of the West Indies felt it important to maintain European customs.

Sexual relations between whites and blacks, if not completely condoned, were more socially acceptable in British West Indian society than in the American South. Planters, poor whites, and overseers in the islands not only slept with (and raped) their female slaves but kept them openly as mistresses. The mulatto children of these unions were sometimes granted their freedom and occasionally were even baptized and educated. In the American South, by contrast, mixed children were almost invariably kept as slaves.

Over time, the mulattoes of the British West Indies came to constitute another caste, separate from both blacks and whites. Those who remained slaves were given the favored, indoor jobs of domestic servants. Although no longer slaves, freed mulattoes were still subject to slave law, not English law. They could not vote, hold office, take certain jobs, or own a significant plot of land. Eventually, as emancipation created the opportunity for the development of a middle class, many mulattoes became lawyers, merchants, and journalists. As the 19th century progressed, those professions provided access to political careers, and even before the 1834 Act of Emancipation, there were mulattoes in the Jamaican House of Assembly.

This 1667 engraving depicts a West Indian sugar plantation. The argument that blacks were constitutionally better suited than whites to endure hard labor under the torrid Caribbean sun was one line of reasoning used by the planters to justify slavery.

Moulin 2. Fourneaux 3. Formes 4. Vinaigrerie 5. Cannes de Suicre SVCRERIE 6. Gros Cocos, p. 111 7. Latanir 8. Pajomirioba 9. Choux Caraibes 10. Cases de Negres 11 Figuir. 135.

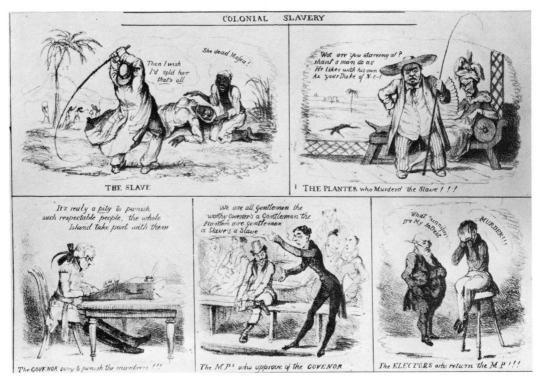

Several aspects of the West Indian plantation system unintentionally allowed blacks some means of cultural and economic independence. In a practice known as provisional planting, slaves were given small plots of land on which to grow their own food; they were allowed to sell at their own marketplace anything beyond what was used for their own needs. This system gave the slave some control over his own livelihood and, it has been argued, a greater degree of self-respect than the American slave could hope to sustain.

To a certain extent, the restraints that denied West Indian slaves religious instruction, education, decent housing, and food enabled (or forced) them to preserve a good deal of their native African culture. Although many learned some English in order to communicate with their masters, most retained their African dialects. Traditional dances—such as the Calenda, the Chica, and the Juba—and songs survived, although hollow-log drums were confiscated by the British, who feared the slaves would use them to

White male planters believed they had a natural right to both the enjoyment and abuse of black female slaves. This political cartoon from 1830 depicts the attitudes and forces that conspired to condone such brutality.

African blacks had developed a complex vocal style with great tonal range as well as a sophisticated use of drums and an orchestra; West Indian blacks built upon this musical foundation. Here, a rather naive drawing shows Trinidadian slaves in celebration.

spread news of pending revolts. Funeral rights remained elaborate; West Africans believed both in ancestor worship and in a peaceful afterlife in the mountains of Africa. (This latter belief drove many slaves to suicide.)

For many years the British colonists refused to admit the slaves into their Protestant churches. Catholic French, Spanish, and Portuguese slaveholders, on the other hand, were eager to baptize their slaves into Catholicism. The only Protestant group that made any early efforts to convert their slaves was the Quakers; their efforts were frowned upon by the white community, however, and in Barbados, for example, Quakers were fined for bringing blacks to meeting. By the late 17th century, however, island governments were calling upon the planters to instruct and educate the more intelligent of their slaves, reassuring them that no slave would become free by becoming a Christian. Missionaries who arrived from Great Britain to minister to these slaves "of ignorance, of sin, and of Satan" were instructed not to plant seeds of discontent in the spirits of the blacks, lest they should then demand their freedom.

Even after various Christian groups undertook the task of conversion, black slaves continued to practice their West African religions. Eventually, Catholic elements, such as the veneration of saints, would combine with elements of the West African spirit-possession cults to form *voodoo* and similar Afro-

Christian religious hybrids. These sects share a strong belief in the working of spirits in the material world (called *myal* in Jamaica) and in ritual forms of magic and propitiation (called *obeah* in Jamaica). These religions continue to thrive on the islands and among communities of West Indian Americans.

Through the first half of the 18th century, the British West Indies prospered, largely as a result of the ever-expanding sugar market. Wealthy planters and Church of England ministers saw to the establishment of a number of excellent secondary schools in Bermuda. In 1730, Codrington College, the first college of consequence, was founded in Barbados. The Peace of Utrecht, an Anglo-Spanish peace and commercial agreement signed in 1713, made the West Indies the locus of depots for British trade with Spanish America, providing yet another source of prosperity. As a group, the West Indian islands played a vital role in the commercial life of the British Empire, supplying a variety of tropical products and purchasing from Great Britain almost all necessary manufactured goods.

During this time of prosperity, the West Indian islands were to a great extent self-governing, with most islands possessing a legislature consisting of a governor as the Crown's representative, a council, and an assembly. Collectively, the islands maintained a strong lobby in Parliament and, in their vigorous suing for increased autonomy, the islands anticipated many of the core issues of the American Revolution. When the War of Independence did break out, West Indian opinion was generally sympathetic to the patriots' cause. Throughout the war the West Indies became even more hostile to the proprietary attitudes of Great Britain, and a relative calm was restored only after the war, when American royalists, seeking asylum from the new nation, came to the islands to fill government positions.

Toward Emancipation

Although British planters were reluctant to acknowledge them, slave uprisings did occur in the West Indies. It is known that seven slave revolts were staged

Because whites justified slavery, in part, with the rationalization that as heathens, or non-Christians, blacks had no souls, events like this mass baptism of slaves in Jamaica in 1791 caused an uproar.

In African religions, ritual, or direct action rather than contemplation, is the most common means of communication with sacred spirits. In the West Indies, blacks often fused the elements of African and Christian religions.

on the British islands between 1640 and 1713, and at least another six major conspiracies were discovered in the planning stages and effectively thwarted. Revolts were most frequent on Jamaica, where the relative isolation of the large plantations and the possibility of escape to the mountains bolstered hopes of success.

However, even in Jamaica, slave revolts were ultimately ineffectual. In many cases a loyal slave betrayed the rebellion to his or her master, a bitter irony that only underscores the atmosphere of fear and intimidation in which the slave population lived. On the whole, slave uprisings caused significantly less damage than natural disasters and epidemics. White society remained fairly secure until the beginning of the 19th century, when the winds of change that were sweeping through Europe began to be felt by opponents of oppression all around the world.

The success of the American Revolution of 1776 had helped to inspire the French to overthrow their monarchy. The French Revolution, in its turn, with its call for liberty, equality, and fraternity, provided the example for the successful revolution in St. Domingue (now known as Haiti) that culminated in 1804 with a proclamation of independence. Under the leadership of the self-educated ex-slave Toussaint L'Ouverture and the black general Jean-Jacques Dessalines, black islanders rose in rebellion against minority white rule and took over the island. Their assertion of human rights and freedom caused many white West Indians on the other islands to admit the possibility of large-scale revolution and the collapse of the prevailing social structure.

Just as the French Revolution had inspired the slaves of Haiti to overthrow the cruel yoke of oppression, so did it plant the seeds of reform in the minds of England's liberals and radicals. British writers such as Thomas Paine, William Godwin, and Mary Wollstonecraft responded vigorously to "the spirit of the age." Poets such as William Wordsworth and William Blake, later dubbed Romantics, were stimulated by "the beauty of promise" to joyously anticipate the imminent birth of a new and just world. Antislavery propagandists such as William Naish made emotional appeals to the British public, such as this passage from his pamphlet entitled *Reasons for Using East India Sugar*:

> May every man, before he indulges his appetite with the blood-bought luxury, reflect upon the price it cost. Not eight pence, or ten pence, or twelve pence, or fourteen pence the pound only; but groans, and wounds, and death. . . . And then let him swallow his beverage with what appetite he may.

Over the next three decades, pressures for reform both at home in England and in the British colonies grew until they could no longer be ignored. In spite of protests from merchants, slave traders, and the British population in the West Indies, in 1834 Parliament passed a bill that abolished slavery in all British colonies.

Although most slave uprisings in the British West Indies failed, some slaves succeeded in escaping to unoccupied areas of the islands, where they lived as refugees.

The Lingering Costs of Freedom

The Act of Emancipation abolished slavery in the British Empire, liberating a total of approximately 700,000 slaves. In order to stave off an expected economic crisis with the elimination of a slave labor force and to help ease the blacks' transition to a free people, the emancipation bill set up a system of mandatory temporary apprenticeship. This period was intended to be one in which blacks would be prepared for full freedom by a series of social reforms. However, many of the planters saw this interim stage as a perfect opportunity to squeeze as much work out of the freed slaves as could be gotten. The blacks resented this further abuse, and in 1838, the apprenticeship system ended, two years earlier than originally scheduled.

Although deprived of slavery's systems of provisional planting and of allowances, through which they had been granted some degree of market experience, rent-free gardens, and supplies of fish and meat, the black community of the British West Indies rapidly became an independent peasantry. In the state of being "full free," they established villages, raised their own food, and sold their labor to planters now desperate for workers. Land, for most blacks, was symbolic of freedom. Very few wanted to return to work on another man's land, even for a wage, but other opportunities were limited.

Emancipation marked the start of a gradual shift of economic and political power from a dominant white minority to a black and mulatto majority. The transition was not easy for either group. The plantation system had always been inefficient (the plow was not introduced to Jamaica until 1830), but the inefficiency had been masked by slavery and by preferential treatment of West Indian sugar on the British market. In 1846, Britain passed the Sugar Duties Act, and the second of the West Indian economic crutches was taken away. This legislation reduced the difference in the duties (essentially taxes levied on imports) charged in Great Britain on foreign and British-grown sugar and provided for complete equalization of duties in 1851.

On July 1, 1801, the former slave Toussaint L'Ouverture proclaimed the constitution of the independent republic of Haiti.

(A second act deferred equalization until 1854.) Faced with increased production costs, the planters began to encourage the immigration of cheap labor in the form of indentured servants from China and India. This rather unimaginative attempt at economic reorganization deprived West Indian blacks of jobs on the plantations.

The British West Indian economy and social structure had suffered an enormously disruptive blow with the demise of slavery, and the islands entered the 20th century in a state of sustained economic crisis. The 1840s had been a period of widespread bankruptcy and financial chaos; the 1850s brought drought and epidemic; the 1860s, episodes of rioting. The traditional agricultural society was unable to absorb the increasing black and mulatto population, leading to both emigration and the growth of urban areas and a predominantly mulatto middle class. Changes were slow in coming, however; island society was still largely based on a rigid hierarchy of class and race, and most of the

Engravings of scenes such as this one, where slaves in Jamaica are being forced to power a water wheel, led such groups as the Society for Effecting the Abolition of the Slave Trade to call for the extinction of a practice "no plea of policy or interest can justify."

Following the abolition of slavery, British planters began to import Chinese and East Indians as a source of cheap labor.

islands still depended on a one-crop economy. Finally, the development of beet sugar in Europe forced the West Indies to look toward other crops and to develop other natural resources. (Today, for example, rice is the main crop in Guyana; Jamaicans grow bananas and export bauxite, the principle ore of aluminum.) The transition to more flexible and diverse economies is still not complete. Large corporations and a few wealthy families still control much of the islands' acreage, and most residents still remain poor.

The worldwide depression of the 1930s greatly aggravated the West Indies' long-standing problems of unemployment, underemployment, low wages, and ineffective governments. A wave of strikes and labor actions that began in 1935 on the Leeward Islands spread southward, culminating in widespread rioting on Jamaica and Trinidad in 1937 and 1938. In 1938 a British Royal Commission of Inquiry sent to the West Indies concluded that the region would benefit from intensified agricultural research, the expansion of social services and educational facilities, and a greater degree of self-government. The commission also noted that "the cumulative effect of education, the press, wireless, the spectacle of the standards of living of white people, and the reports of West Indians who have lived and worked abroad, particularly in the United States of America, has been to create a demand for better conditions of work and life."

Out of the riots grew the first enduring labor organizations in the British West Indies. Between 1939 and 1945, workers in the West Indies formed 65 trade unions; legislation was passed to institute departments of labor and to establish means for regulating labor disputes.

The development of autonomous governments was slower. In the years following World War II some ad-

This Kingston, Jamaica, street was left littered with debris following a riot there in 1938. As their economic situation worsened in the early decades of the 20th century, the West Indies were often the site of civil unrest.

vances toward representative government and the gradual introduction of universal adult suffrage were made. (The importance of the latter reform is made obvious in the case of Trinidad, where, in 1934, only 25,000 people of an adult population of 400,000 had the right to vote.) Complete ministerial systems (with the powers for a significant measure of internal self-government) were established in Trinidad, Jamaica, and Barbados. In the latter two islands, the lower chambers of the legislatures were made elective, and in most of the colonies local inhabitants were elected to ministries. In the early 1960s, several organizations devoted to the promotion of common social, cultural, and economic affairs among the islands were established.

The colonies of the British West Indies hoped to form a federation with eventual commonwealth status. (This means that the islands would be self-governing, autonomous political units, voluntarily associated with Great Britain and recognizing the monarchy as the only legal bond between them.) On February 23, 1956, a conference of island delegates in London approved a plan of union. In August 1956, recognizing the growing importance of West Indian feelings of nationality and solidarity, Parliament enacted the British Caribbean Federation Act, and on July 31, 1957, the West Indies Federation was established.

Though provisions were made for a common legislature, with an elected house of representatives and an appointed senate, Trinidad and Tobago refused to join the federation, and in September 1961, Jamaica withdrew because of dissatisfaction with its representation in the legislature. As a result of this dissension, Britain dissolved the West Indies Federation, although the common services it provided were continued. (Under the federation, Britain had retained the power of legislating in matters of defense, external relations, and maintenance of financial stability and credit.) While the other islands reverted to their former status, in 1962 Jamaica and Trinidad and Tobago became independent members of the British Commonwealth. In 1966, British Guiana (Guyana) and Barbados became independent republics, and in 1967, Antigua, St. Kitts, Nevis, Anguilla, Dominica, St. Lucia, and Grenada joined together to form the West Indies Associated States with Great Britain. St. Vincent joined them in 1969. (An associated state has the power of complete internal self-government and the option of becoming independent at any time. Until it does, Britain retains responsibility for external affairs.) In 1973, the Bahamas became an independent republic, followed in 1974 by Grenada, in 1978 by Dominica, in 1979 by St. Lucia and St. Vincent, and in 1981 by Antigua and Belize.

THE FIRST WAVE

The first great wave of West Indian immigration took place between 1900 and 1930. During that time, between 80,000 and 90,000 blacks from the British West Indies arrived in the United States. The height of this immigration occurred between 1911 and 1924. In those years, 70 percent of all employed persons entering the United States from the British West Indies were professional, white-collar, or skilled workers. The majority of this group were mulatto; 3 out of every 4 were between the ages of 14 and 44. By the middle of the century, more than half of all West Indian immigrants were of the professional or skilled worker class.

This educated, talented, and youthful group of immigrants was the product of a unique set of circumstances that had created a sizable black middle class alongside the existent mulatto one. During much of the 19th century, blacks in the British West Indies constituted over 90 percent of the island populations. So large a group had to be allowed to perform a wide variety of jobs in order for the British West Indian society to function. From the late 19th century on, blacks were to be found as government administrators, businessmen, professionals, and craftsmen.

There is no way to determine the total number of British West Indians, both black and mulatto, who en-

A public washtub in Kingstown, St. Vincent. Poor living and sanitary conditions were common in West Indian towns and villages in the late 1800s and early 1900s.

tered the United States in the early years of the 20th century. The U.S. Immigration and Naturalization Service recorded newcomers as being either of the "West Indian race"—the people so classified were predominantly mulatto—or, if their skin was darker, as members of the "African race." This group was probably more numerous and less educated or skilled than those considered "West Indian," although a certain number of blacks were members of the West Indian middle class.

There is a further problem with accurately establishing the number of British West Indians who came to America during the first great wave of immigration. While the U.S. Census and Bureau of Immigration distinguished British West Indians from Puerto Ricans and Cubans, they did not distinguish them from French, Dutch, and Spanish West Indians. However, there is good reason to believe that between 80 and 90 percent of West Indian immigrants to America during this time were from the British West Indies. In 1910, a census report documented that only 3 percent of all foreign-born blacks over 10 years of age could not speak English. In 1920 and again in 1930, only two percent of this population could not speak the language. Although the figures imply that a small number of French, Dutch, and Spanish West Indians had learned English, they also suggest that English-speaking West Indians constituted a majority of immigrants from the islands.

Beginning in about 1900, steamship routes connected the West Indian islands to ports on the East Coast of the United States, making New York, Massachusetts, and Florida the main points of entry for West Indian immigrants. New York City became the home of 65 percent of all immigrant blacks in America. In the 1930s, Harlem was one-quarter West Indian, and there were also large West Indian communities in Brooklyn.

A New Way of Life

West Indians came to North America primarily in search of economic opportunity. The West Indian islands were small, isolated, and, in spite of the gains made by the mulatto and black middle class, socially and economically stratified. Great Britain's adoption of free trade in 1846 had completed their economic ruin, and for the majority of the population opportunity remained limited. Working conditions for the island laborers were often terrible, leading to workers' riots in Jamaica (1902, 1912, 1924), Trinidad (1902), British Guiana (1905), St. Lucia (1908), Antigua (1918), Barbuda (1918), British Honduras (1919), and Tobago (1919). Agricultural communities were plagued by persistent poverty, and hurricanes and other natural disasters often destroyed peasant farmers' livelihoods. The islanders had limited ability to effect significant change, as only a very few were allowed to exercise political rights. In 1938 on the island of Barbados, for example, only 18 percent of the adult male population had the right to vote, and most of those were wealthy and white.

As transportation became more accessible and less expensive, more and more West Indians left to seek their fortunes in the United States and Canada. When manpower grew short during the first and second world wars, the United States recruited West Indians for factory and farm work. (It is estimated that by 1945 there were more than 50,000 West Indians in the United States as temporary laborers.) In the 10 years that followed World War I, the United States enjoyed a period of prosperity and boisterous optimism—the Roaring Twenties—that acted as a magnet to islanders seeking a better life. In Ira Reid's *Negro Immigrant*, one Bahamian recalls being convinced to come to the United States by fellow islanders who had already emigrated:

> Home returning pilgrims told exaggerated tales of their fame and fortune in the "promised land." As convincing evidence to their claims, they dressed flashily and spent American dollars lavishly and prodigally. Those American dollars had a bewitching charm for a country lad who worked for wages ranging from 36 to 50 cents a day.

Once arrived in the United States, West Indians tended to establish tightly knit communities, a practice that owed as much to American racism as to their desire to live in close proximity to family, friends, and

A group of West Indian women at Ellis Island, circa 1900. West Indian immigrants differed in two significant ways from the great mass of immigrants who were entering the United States around that time— they were black, and they spoke English.

countrymen. As was the case with American blacks, discrimination prevented black West Indians from moving into predominantly white neighborhoods. While daily life in exclusively West Indian neighborhoods did help West Indians to maintain their ties to the homeland and to assert their ethnic distinctiveness, it also excluded them from full participation in American society.

West Indian immigrants were often frustrated in their attempts to practice the trades in which they were proficient. Time and again, skilled workers, such as bricklayers, mechanics, and tailors, and white-collar workers, such as clerks and accountants, found themselves unable to obtain a good job in their field because of their color. In historian Ira Reid's *The Negro Immigrant*, a skilled worker from the Virgin Islands described his shame at having to perform unskilled labor:

> At home I was a clerk. My beginning salary might have been fifteen dollars per month. I was led to despise the tasks of the porter. . . . Care not how small the salary was, I had a position. Now I have to work at a . . . menial job. . . . Usually, my first position is that of being a porter or an elevator runner. I cannot write home and inform my friends of the nature of my work.

In spite of such frustrations, most immigrants were financially better off as unskilled workers in America than they had been as skilled workers at home. Relatively few West Indians stayed in menial jobs for long. Compared to other immigrant groups, an unusually large number of West Indians were literate. Postemancipation British West Indian society had constructed a system of education and religious instruction that had produced an anglicized African with the skills and information needed to succeed in a white-ruled culture; as a result, in the years between 1911 and 1924, 99 percent of British West Indian immigrants were able to read and write English. A black American journalist named George S. Schuyler noted the newcomers' "enterprise in business, their pushfulness."

Father Harrison, right, and Father Shelton Haile Bishop, left, greet parishioners after Easter Sunday service at St. Phillip's Protestant Episcopal Church in Harlem, New York City, in the late 1930s. West Indian immigrants transported many of the institutions they had known at home to their neighborhoods in North America.

Those who came to the United States as unskilled laborers attended trade schools and learned new skills. Those with entrepreneurial skills often opened up small businesses, such as retail stores. This common practice gave rise to a popular saying in Harlem: "As soon as a West Indian gets ten cents above a beggar, he opens a business." Lawyers, doctors, journalists, and other professionals, who were often excluded from practicing in the white community, found satisfaction in serving the black community. It is estimated that up to one-third of the black professionals in New York in the first part of the 20th century were West Indian.

To facilitate their success in a society that was hostile to blacks, those immigrants who had once been a part of the West Indian middle class banded together and formed mutual-benefit and homeowners' associations. The Antillian Realty Company, for example, was a very successful black real estate firm, with holdings totaling $750,000. The Association of Barbadian Homeowners and Businessmen helped its members buy houses, gave loans for the opening of small businesses, and even offered a college scholarship for a qualifying member of its youth group.

Racism and America

Having come from a colonial society in which one's class standing was ultimately more important than one's color, the typical West Indian was confused by American racial prejudice. Though racism did exist in the British West Indies, with mulattoes regarded as being in some way superior to darker-skinned blacks and whites as superior to both, it had not prevented black citizens from earning a place in the middle class and from being accorded respect for their achievement. Thus, a black Trinidadian could say of his status at home:

> There was never any question of my being a
> gentleman. I was by the fault of a circumstance,
> of the "upper middle class." I was at all times
> addressed as Mr. even by my elders and quite
> naturally by domestics who suffer intolerably
> from the devastating and disgusting effects of the
> class system that exists in the islands. I was
> rather accustomed to homage and deference.

A store workers' strike in Harlem in 1936. West Indians were often at the forefront of the black labor movement.

During the 1920s and 1930s, American blacks were not accustomed to "homage and deference." West Indians were shocked by southern segregation policies and northern racism.

> The whole situation down South filled me with bitterness and contempt," said one student quoted in *The Negro Immigrant*. "The utter ridiculousness of the sign in the cars 'Whites to the front, colored to the rear.' The girl that pointed it out to me was so amused for I could not stop reading it and laughing. . . . It did not seem possible to me that such conditions could exist in one of the centers of civilization.

Until World War II, the relationship between West Indian and American blacks was often antagonistic. West Indian immigrants were generally status conscious and often looked down on American blacks for their lack of education. They perhaps failed to realize that the blacks who had moved to northern cities from the rural South had come from an environment that had offered little in the way of economic or educational opportunity. (Nor was racism exclusively a southern problem. Blacks in the north rarely enjoyed the same educational or economic opportunities as whites.) Partly as a result of this misunderstanding, West Indians tended to socialize exclusively with other West Indians and not with American blacks. In the 1930s, 98 percent of the West Indian women at American colleges married West Indian men. Marriage to an American black was considered a step down the social ladder. American blacks responded to this cultural snobbery by mocking West Indians, calling them "monkey-chasers," "Jew-maicans," "Garveyites," and "cockneys." "The West Indian Blues," a popular song in Harlem during the height of West Indian immigration, illustrates this tendency to stereotype.

> Done give up de bestes' job,
> A runnin' elevator,
> I told my boss "Mon" I'd be back
> Sometime soon or later.

When I git back to this great land,
You better watch me Harvey
'Cause 'm gonna be a great big "Mon"
Like my fren' Marcus Garvey.

"The West Indian Blues" and songs like it demonstrate some of the more obvious points of contention that existed between American and West Indian blacks. American blacks were suspicious of the West Indian dislike for menial labor, perhaps failing to understand fully the social environment from which the immigrants had come. While a significant portion of black West Indians had once held jobs of some consequence on their native islands, American blacks had most probably been excluded from all but menial jobs for all of their lives. The apparent ability of West Indians to quickly better their economic status in America added further cause for resentment.

Whites and blacks unite at a meeting of the Communist party in 1930. During the hard times of the Great Depression, the Communist party's message of working-class solidarity appealed to many immigrant workers.

West Indians responded to such cultural tensions and antagonisms by establishing organizations designed to improve relations between themselves and American blacks. In the 1920s, the West Indian Reform Association, the West Indian Committee in America, and the Foreign-Born Citizens' Alliance sought in various ways to develop "cordial relations between West Indians and colored Americans." By the late 1930s and early 1940s, partly because of decreased immigration during the Great Depression and World War II, tensions between the two groups had lessened considerably, and during the civil rights movement of the 1960s, West Indians and black Americans worked together toward common goals.

Sojourners in America

Many of the West Indian immigrants who came to the United States in the first few decades of the 20th century displayed what is sometimes known as a sojourner mentality. They insisted that they had come to America only to earn their fortunes and that they would someday return to the land of their birth. Distance and nostalgia made them remember the islands as tropical paradises and helped them forget the economic hardships that had driven them away. Even after 20 or 30 years in the United States, older immigrants could be heard planning their return trips home—trips many of them would never make.

Largely because of this sojourner mentality, West Indian immigrants in the first decades of this century tended to avoid obtaining U.S. citizenship. In 1920 only 13 percent of all male foreign-born blacks were naturalized citizens, and in 1930 the number had increased to merely 28.3 percent. Wishing to increase their political clout, both native blacks and naturalized citizens exerted steady pressure on the nonnaturalized to become citizens and to vote. In 1937 the *New York Amsterdam News*, Harlem's foremost weekly paper, carried this boxed statement on its masthead:

> Become a citizen—prepare to vote. The Negro's strength in affairs which concern his very existence

is gauged by the ballot. If you are not a citizen, become one. The U.S. Naturalization Service has division offices at 641 Washington Street, Manhattan, Canal 6-2100.

In spite of this and similar pleas, many West Indians remained reluctant to become citizens until the 1930s, when there was a rise in the number of British West Indians who applied for citizenship. Although some became United States citizens as a natural consequence of the process of social assimilation, others sought citizenship in order to qualify for jobs and to receive the benefits of federal employment and relief programs during the depression.

In North America, West Indians who had belonged to the Church of England at home usually became members of the Episcopal church, the American branch of Protestantism most closely related to the Anglican sect. The church served the community as the center of its social and cultural life as well as the focus of its religious existence. Among other things, Episcopal houses of worship were used as the meeting places for patriotic activities that helped to reaffirm the West Indians' attachment to the British crown. On May 12, 1937, St. Ambrose Parish in New York City sponsored a ball to celebrate the coronation of George VI as king of England. Printed invitations gave the entrance price in British currency. More than 5,000 people attended, and the *New York Amsterdam News* said of the affair that

Hubert Henry Harrison, born in St. Croix, the Virgin Islands, was a prominent Harlem political leader in the 1920s. Like many West Indian–American political leaders of the day, Harrison was a Socialist.

> Rockland Palace was a riot of colors and bunting. Most eye-hitting were the Union Jack and Colonial flags, which were set on a blue background with white stars. While plenty of liquor flowed freely among the exuberant celebrators, not one of the 5,000 was inebriated or boisterous—which was a tribute to the tone of the affair.

That West Indian immigrants should engage in such assertions of nationalistic feeling for a colonial empire that had enslaved their ancestors may seem puzzling, as might their wish to retain British citizenship. Such behavior is more easily understood when one considers the shock and dismay felt by West Indians at the sweeping racial prejudice they encountered. Those who had been members of the middle class greatly resented their new status. To some extent, the West Indians' loyalty to Great Britain helped distinguish them from the much-abused American black population, and it also dramatically expressed their disappointment in a society so unjust to all blacks.

In reality, the West Indians' attitude toward Britain contained more than a trace of irony, and it was in the dance and musical traditions that came into being soon after emancipation that much of this cultural anxiety was expressed. *The Newer Caribbean—Decolonialization, Democracy, and Development,* a collection of essays on West Indian culture and history, explains that not long after the 1834 Act of Emancipation, carnival and Christmas celebrations emerged as primarily black rituals. These celebrations provided an occasion of cultural expression for a people still largely illiterate. Through the "mas" band and its various "mases," black West Indians gave musical form to the psychological and emotional tensions of their world. Emancipation was celebrated with *Canboulay* and *Jon Canoe,* colorful theatrical pageants combining music and dance. *Shango* bands and Moko Jumbee paraded African heritage, and Jamet and Devil bands expressed a fierce rejection of colonial society. The drama of John Bull (a British national symbol comparable to Uncle Sam) acted out the blacks' hatred of the colonizer, while "fancy bands," in which people dressed like the king and queen, acted out the blacks' identification with the British.

West Indian immigrants continued to practice many non-British customs in America. One of them was the Harvest Festival. In the West Indies during the month of October, it was customary to bring one's best produce to the local church. On Harvest Sunday the church was decorated with fruits and vegetables of all kinds. The minister would say special prayers, the congregation would sing hymns celebrating the

(continued on page 57)

AWARENESS AND PRIDE

In Brooklyn, New York, a young boy (overleaf) joins dancers in this West Indian parade, a popular event at which West Indian Americans gather to celebrate their heritage. Members of the community (right and below) enjoy gathering to design and construct elaborate floats and costumes.

The West Indian carnival tradition, born more than a century ago out of a newly liberated community's need for self-expression, continues to thrive. At the West Indian Labor Day festival, costumes of fantasy, color, and light attract and astonish New Yorkers of all races and religions.

West Indian Americans are becoming increasingly involved in politics both local and universal. A West Indian man (above) sports a T-shirt that announces concern about the pride of the worldwide black community. Marchers (above right) hold an anti-drug-abuse sign reflecting an awareness of drugs as a family problem. David Dinkins (bottom right) joins supporters at the 1989 West Indian Labor Day parade. Dinkins was elected mayor of New York City in November 1989.

These West Indian American children are the proud heirs to their parents' significant achievements in North America.

(continued from page 48)

season, and the next day the collected food would be sold or distributed to the poor. During the 1930s, St. Cyprian's, in the Columbus Hill district of Harlem, turned the Harvest Festival into a street bazaar at which food and goods were sold to benefit the church. The tradition lived on, with local modifications, in other neighborhoods as well.

Many other West Indian traditions were maintained in the United States. Both marriages and funerals remained huge events. As one writer for the *Baltimore Afro-American* put it, "The big question in West Indian circles is not who you marry but how you marry." Wakes were also occasions for celebration. In the West Indies, friends and family would stay up all night with the dead, praying, feasting, and socializing. On some of the islands celebrations with drinking and dancing continued for a week after the death. In the United States, these funeral customs were continued, albeit on a somewhat smaller scale. Friends were served food and drink in the deceased's home after the burial, and it was not unusual for funeral celebrations to continue uninterrupted throughout a weekend.

Afro-Christian religions also survived in West Indian communities in North America. Immigrants from Haiti continued to practice voodoo, a folk religion that combines Catholic traditions with beliefs and practices derived from the spirit-possession cults of West Africa. Similar Afro-Christian sects that had developed on the other West Indian islands (for example, shango on Trinidad) also traveled with the immigrants to America. These religions share a belief in magic and in a world of gods who possess their worshipers in rituals. Magic rests on the belief that there exists a mystic connection between certain ritual acts performed by humans and the results they desire. These acts temporarily harness the power of the supernatural and persuade it to work on the believer's behalf. For believers, magic rituals form an important part of daily religious life. For example, fetishes, objects made of wood or cloth and worn around the neck or placed around the home, are believed to contain the spirits of great natural forces and are invoked for their help in granting the believer's prayer. Other activities include the casting of spells and the lighting of black candles in cemeteries in honor of Baron Samedi, lord of the underworld. *Lao*, or gods, and the dead are the *Invisibles* upon whom magic cannot be used. The Invisibles are seen as the principles of grandeur, pride, and power and are propitiated by an individual's changing his or her own life for the better. The Invisibles haunt a believer because they represent his or her unused faculties; until he or she undergoes a grueling initiation into voodoo, which involves surviving various forms of possession by the gods, he or she will not be at rest. Interestingly, the lao retain African tribal identities long lost to the black West Indians.

Agitators and Activists

While many British West Indians in America concentrated on preserving a sense of their island identity and on earning enough money to enable them to return home, another group reacted to life in America in a very different way. A large minority of West Indians became politically active and earned themselves a reputation as "agitators." Much of the immigrants' political activity was a result of their anger at the forms of discrimination and prejudice they encountered in America. Their political activism may also be attributed in part to a history of political participation, although limited, in the 19th-century British imperial system.

In Harlem in the 1920s and 1930s, West Indian immigrants became famous as street-corner orators, and the reputation of the West Indians for political activism gave rise to a popular joke: Question: What's the definition of radical? Answer: An overeducated West Indian without a job.

Possessed of firsthand experience of a society in which blacks were the majority and held a wide variety of jobs, West Indians became active in labor unions, leading the fight for better pay and more job opportunities for all blacks. They helped develop collective bargaining for black workers and organized boycotts of stores that would not hire blacks. West Indian women led the successful fight for black women to be allowed to work in the garment industry. This was an

Labor leader Frank Crosswaith was one of the West Indian immigrants who assumed a position of leadership in New York City's black community in the 1930s.

especially important victory because so few industrial jobs were open to women in the 1920s and 1930s.

In organized city politics, West Indians tended to favor the Socialist and Democratic parties. They formed cohesive special interest groups in both New York and Boston and often held the balance of power in many Harlem precincts. Hubert H. Harrison, an immigrant from St. Croix in the Virgin Islands, was a prominent Socialist leader, an outspoken critic of the injustices of American society, and a defender of the "Negro's racial heritage." In 1917 he organized the Liberty League, based in Harlem, and founded its newspaper, the *Voice*. It was Harrison who offered Marcus Garvey his first public platform in New York City on June 12, 1917, at the Bethel African Methodist Episcopal Church. Harrison later helped Garvey edit the *Negro World*, and in 1917 he published *The Negro and the Nation*. Reverend Ethelred Brown, Richard B. Moore, and Frank R. Crosswaith, all West Indian immigrants, ran as Socialists or Communists for the New York City Board of Aldermen, the state assembly, and the U.S. Congress. None were successful, but they helped to set an example of political involvement for both the West Indian and American black community.

British West Indians in Canada

At the same time that Harlem was being populated by West Indian immigrants, Canada was welcoming its

Manhattan Borough president Hulan Jack (center, with scissors), a West Indian immigrant from St. Lucia, cuts the ribbon at the opening of a Food Family supermarket in Harlem in the 1950s. The success of West Indians in politics and business often made them the targets of resentment of American-born blacks.

share of newcomers from the islands. Most of the immigrants to Canada were Jamaican; others hailed from the Bahamas, British Guiana, Bermuda, and St. Vincent. The majority of this population were unskilled laborers. Recruited in the West Indies by labor agents for major companies and given subsidized passages to Sydney, Nova Scotia, they found work in steel mills, coal mines, and on the railroads. Others moved on to find employment in the shipyards of Halifax and Collingwood. Eventually, many of the workers migrated from Nova Scotia to Toronto and other urban areas, where they found jobs similar to those available for blacks in New York City at the time—as bellhops, porters, and domestic servants, for example.

Many of these West Indian immigrants had bypassed the United States because they had felt that their experience in a British society would serve them better in Canada. Although not completely without prejudice, Canadian society was certainly less racist than U.S. society in the first half of the 20th century. But as in New York City, West Indian blacks in Canada experienced cultural conflict with the resident black community.

Many of the blacks living in Toronto in the years before the First World War were the descendants of freed slaves who had come north from the American South, but blacks who fled to Canada found freedom, not equality. Nevertheless, over time the black community in Toronto experienced some degree of economic and social success, largely through an unstated policy of accommodation and integration. Blacks held positions of responsibility in nearly all religious, civil, and military organizations.

The West Indian immigrants who arrived in Toronto after World War I were seen by other blacks as a potential threat to the status quo. Most of the immigrants were unskilled laborers, and the natives—better educated and more successful in comparison—looked down on them. The few black West Indian professionals who did immigrate to Toronto found it difficult to set up practice because the native blacks jealously guarded their hard-won positions.

Still, similarities in the pattern of West Indian assimilation into U.S. and Canadian societies can be seen. Although West Indians in Canada initially felt a sense of rivalry with immigrants from other islands, they were united in considering themselves in some way superior to Canadian blacks. West Indians organized separate clubs, attended Anglican churches, supported cricket matches, and, as in the United States, supported the early Back to Africa movement. For example, in 1921, the African Orthodox church was founded in Sydney, Nova Scotia, by George A. McGuire, a native of Antigua and a former follower of Garvey's. Although few Canadian blacks either desired or were granted admission to this black nationalist offshoot of Methodism, its single parish thrived. From 1928 to 1936, under the leadership of Archdeacon Dixon Egbert Philips, a Tobagan native and Garveyite, the African Orthodox church flourished. In 1940, a Cuban-born black, the Reverend George A. Frances, arrived to see the church through even more profitable years.

Canadian blacks were not overwhelmingly drawn to Marcus Garvey and his uncompromising message. When they denounced his work, Garvey accused them of "Uncle Tomism." Nevertheless, in 1936, years after his deportation from the United States, Garvey held an International Convention of the Negro Peoples of the World in Toronto; his subsequent efforts at establishing a Garveyite school in Canada were abruptly aborted by his death in 1940. In 1967, some West Indians in Canada revived the United Negro Improvement Association (UNIA). A larger group, however, put together what became the Toronto United Negro Association and an allied credit union. This organization was more conservative in its racial policy than was the UNIA and worked from the premise that the black man and woman were in Canada to stay. But their differences in policy aside, West Indian groups in Canada and the United States were united by a common belief in black pride and the need to make significant social changes in order to better the lot of blacks in North America.

THE
AUTOBIOGRAPHY
OF AN
EX-COLOURED MAN
JAMES WELDON JOHNSON

First published in 1912 and reprinted in 1927, James Weldon Johnson's novel The Autobiography of an Ex-Coloured Man *exerted a great influence on the writers of the Harlem Renaissance.*

THE HARLEM RENAISSANCE

The 12 years of political and social readjustment in the American South that followed the end of the Civil War in 1865 is known as the Reconstruction. The most vigorous support for a complete restructuring of southern society came from the radical wing of the Republican party, led by Senator Charles Sumner of Massachusetts and Representative Thaddeus Stevens of Pennsylvania, who called for the complete and permanent abolishment of slavery and the passing of laws that would grant equal rights to ex-slaves. The 14th and 15th Amendments, ratified in 1868 and 1870, respectively, granted blacks citizenship and the right to vote. These advances led blacks to expect an overall improvement in both their economic and social status.

However, the widespread corruption of the Reconstruction governments helped dash black hopes. The newly liberated black population was prey to various overt and subtle forms of abuse. From the North came unscrupulous men eager to take control of southern state and municipal governments strictly for the financial rewards such posts offered. Known as "carpetbaggers" for the sort of luggage they typically carried,

With the abolition of slavery, white American society developed new methods of oppressing the black minority. Among these was the perpetuation of the stereotype of the black man as a happy-go-lucky, musical, entertaining but essentially feckless and lazy individual. This stereotype had its roots in the performances of such white entertainers as Thomas "Daddy" Rice, shown in a lithograph from 1830, who donned blackface for their racist (and extremely popular) minstrel shows.

these mercenaries cooperated with a group of exploitative southern politicians known as "scalawags" to gain political power and profit. Carpetbaggers and scalawags appealed largely to freed blacks, making promises they could never fulfill. Their greed helped plunge the southern states into even greater debt and disorder.

While carpetbaggers and scalawags casually used blacks for their own purposes, another group of southern whites feared this new and potentially powerful voting population. Some assumed that the presumed innocence and ignorance of the newly empowered freedmen would soon lead to disaster; others were terrified at the prospect of predominantly black state governments that could be expected to show little sympathy toward ex-slaveholders. In order to regain control of their governments from the black populace, southern whites were not above using terrorism and fraud, particularly once the last federal troops were removed from the South in 1877. During the last 16 years of the 19th century, more than 2,000 blacks were lynched in the United States. By the 1890s, southern states were successfully instituting laws that denied voting privileges to any person who could not meet certain standards of literacy and property ownership, thereby effectively undermining the 14th and 15th amendments. In *Plessy v. Ferguson*, a case involving the segregation of railway cars in some southern states, the U.S. Supreme Court ruled in 1896 that "separate but equal accommodations" were constitutional, a landmark opinion that sanctioned segregation in both the North and the South for almost 60 years. Laws and practices that enforced segregation became known as Jim Crow laws after the song "Jump Jim Crow," made popular in 1828 by the minstrel performer Thomas "Daddy" Rice. Segregation policies and racist feelings were not exclusive to the South. In 1900, race riots broke out in New York City; Springfield, Illinois, witnessed similar disturbances eight years later.

With the outbreak of World War I, blacks experienced renewed hope for equality. Those who chose to join the army were confident that their patriotism would earn them a new respect upon their return from Europe. Those who stayed at home searched for new opportunities. Thousands of blacks left the rural South and found jobs in northern defense factories, which, having stepped up wartime production, were in need of cheap labor. One of the results of this massive population shift, known as the great migration, was an increase in racial tensions in the North over decent housing and employment. Blacks became more vocal about their desire for equal rights; the National Association for the Advancement of Colored People (NAACP) and other civil rights organizations called out for justice. The reactions of white Americans were mixed. The Ku Klux Klan and other white supremacist groups reached a peak of popularity in the North dur-

Other white methods for ensuring that blacks "knew their place" were less subtle. The frequency of lynchings and other violent crimes directed against blacks in the first two decades of the 20th century led the National Association for the Advancement of Colored People to campaign to make lynching a federal offense.

ing the 1920s. At the same time, a significant number of white Americans expressed sympathy with the blacks' desire for equal rights, thus creating a white audience receptive to the words of new black authors. Harlem, a residential section of New York City, became the locus of a population of artists, writers, and intellectuals eager to speak out to both white and black Americans. Their voices formed the core of the movement known as the Harlem Renaissance, which during the 1920s represented not only a flowering of black culture in music, literature, and the visual arts but also an expanding sense of racial consciousness and pride.

Americans as well as fashionable visitors from Europe were drawn to the Harlem speakeasies (the illegal bars that slaked Americans' thirst for alcohol during Prohibition) to hear a new music known as jazz, performed by the likes of Duke Ellington, one of the greatest pianists, composers, and bandleaders of the Jazz

Age. Jazz was a uniquely American synthesis of West African rhythms, improvised melodies, and European harmonic elements. Its improvisational style, a consequence of the interplay of diverse cultural influences, allowed the performer to express the powerful and ambivalent feelings of blacks as they were confronted with life in a white culture.

A Vital Voice

Many of the intellectuals active in the renaissance were either West Indian immigrants or people of West Indian descent. James Weldon Johnson, the elder statesman of the Harlem Renaissance, was born in 1871 in Jacksonville, Florida, to a father born a free man in Virginia and to a mother from the Bahamas. Although the Emancipation Proclamation had been signed fewer than 10 years before Johnson's birth, slavery was but a distant memory for his family. Little is known about his paternal grandparents, but his maternal grandfather had held many important political posts in the Bahamas, including the positions of chief inspector of the police and member of the House of Assembly. Both his parents were well educated; his mother, Helen, taught him and his brother to play piano, and Johnson remembered her reading *David Copperfield* aloud to him when he was about six years old. After obtaining a degree at Atlanta University, Johnson returned to Jacksonville, where he held jobs as a high school principal, newspaper editor, and lawyer. Opportunities for blacks in the South, however, were much too limited for a man as talented and ambitious as Johnson. He and his brother moved to New York City, where, with Bob Cole, they became one of the most popular songwriting teams of the era, producing successful songs for the stage such as "Under the Bamboo Tree" and "Congo Love Song." Johnson had been active in Republican politics, and in 1904 the Roosevelt administration offered him a consular post in Puerto Cabello, Venezuela. He served there and then in Corinto, Nicaragua, until the Democrats returned to office in 1912.

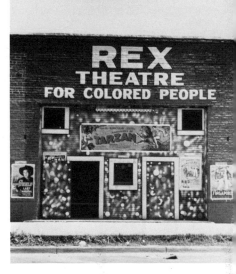

A blacks-only movie theater in Leland, Mississippi, in 1937. The segregation statutes that were the law in many states well into the 20th century ostensibly provided for the creation of separate-but-equal facilities for blacks and whites, but they functioned to deprive blacks of their civil rights and economic opportunity.

By 1920, Harlem was the most heavily populated black residential district in the United States. Poet Paul Laurence Dunbar wrote of its appeal to blacks: "All the days of their lives they had heard about it, and it seemed to them the center of all the glory, all the wealth, and all the freedom of the world."

Although Johnson was an excellent diplomat, his years of foreign service are perhaps most important for the opportunity they afforded him to write *The Autobiography of an Ex-Coloured Man*, a book that anticipated much of the literature of the Harlem Renaissance. *The Autobiography of an Ex-Coloured Man* is a novel about a black man so light skinned that he can pass for white. When the protagonist finds his musical career frustrated because of the color of his skin, he decides to "pass." He does not pretend to be white; he simply stops acting like a black, assumes a place in white society, and people consequently assume that he is white. His strategy is successful for a while; he even marries a white woman, to whom he reveals his secret, but in the end he is unsatisfied and longs for the black community. As a white man, his success has been merely personal and, ultimately, hollow.

Originally published in 1912, nearly a decade before the Harlem Renaissance began, *The Autobiography of an Ex-Coloured Man* was reissued in 1927. Along with *The Souls of Black Folk* by W. E. B. Du Bois, another prominent black intellectual, Johnson's book was one of the most influential works of literature for black intellectuals of the 1920s. *The Autobiography of an Ex-*

Coloured Man was one of the first novels to treat a black man as a complex, thinking character and not merely as a stereotype. By describing the hero's inner spiritual struggle, Johnson laid the groundwork for the issue future black writers would grapple with: how to reconcile the European-based culture of the white American with the unique culture of the black American.

Johnson returned to New York in 1914 and became field secretary of the newly formed NAACP. He served in this post for 4 years and then as its executive secretary for 10. For the rest of his life he continued to exert enormous political and intellectual influence on American society. He changed the NAACP from a small white-led organization to a large black-based lobbying group; he led the fight for antilynching legislation and for a change in segregation policies. In 1915, as editor of the black newspaper *New York Age*, he

The Sam Wooding Orchestra, circa 1925. The genius of black jazz musicians was at the center of the Harlem Renaissance, but at such famous jazz showcases as the Cotton Club only whites were admitted to admire the performers' talents.

founded the "Poetry Corner," a section devoted to poetry by and about blacks. In his preface to the *Book of American Negro Poetry*, an anthology he edited in 1922, Johnson wrote that "the world does not know that a race is great until that race produces great literature. . . . No race that has produced a good literature has ever been looked upon by the world as distinctly inferior."

Others Take Up the Cry

By 1920, American blacks were looking seriously for ways to redefine their place in society. Many had been severely disillusioned by their treatment during World War I. Intellectuals such as Johnson and W. E. B. DuBois had urged blacks to prove their loyalty to their country. Many young black men had answered this call, and the all-black 369th Regiment, nicknamed the

James Weldon Johnson, the elder statesman of the Harlem Renaissance, believed it promised a future of "greater and greater things" for blacks.

Hell Fighters by the French, was the only American regiment to be awarded the French Croix de Guerre. While in France, black American soldiers experienced a lack of racism they had never known before. Yet attitudes in the United States failed to change. The NAACP newspaper *Crisis* obtained and published a secret U.S. government directive that advised French soldiers not to speak or eat with black soldiers or to shake their hands. After the war there was a huge rise in the number of lynchings and race riots all over the country. So, while such blacks as James Weldon Johnson continued to believe in working with whites and within the white system for gradual social change, there arose among the people a more militant philosophy, that of the "New Negro."

Many of the most influential black newspaper owners and journalists of the 1920s were West Indians. One such journalist, a Jamaican named W. A. Domingo, defined the New Negro in the August 1920

The all-black 369th Regiment, nicknamed the Hell Fighters by the French, was the only American regiment in World War I to be awarded the French Croix de Guerre.

issue of the *Messenger* as insisting on "absolute and unequivocal social equality." Until this time, the prevailing philosophy of black rights had been that of educator Booker T. Washington, who believed that blacks should try to educate themselves and to work their way up the economic ladder, prudently accepting the social status assigned them by white society. Domingo's definition of the New Negro directly challenged Washington's notion of accommodation. For example, Domingo believed that because most blacks were members of the working class, they shared some of the same economic interests as the white working class. This made possible interracial tactical alliances, but Domingo's New Negro reserved the right to form black unions when necessary. The New Negro was willing to fight for his rights.

One man who combined the intellectual ideals of the Harlem Renaissance and the political beliefs of the New Negro was the Jamaican writer Claude McKay. McKay had grown up in rural Jamaica in a family of prosperous small farmers. The relative wealth and superior education of the dark-skinned McKays allowed them to claim a social position akin to that of the mulattoes. Claude McKay's father was one of the first black men on the island with enough property to qualify to vote, and his elder brother held the prestigious job of schoolteacher in a neighboring town. Like James Weldon Johnson, McKay grew up surrounded by books and was encouraged in his intellectual explorations. By the time he turned 21 in 1912, he had published 2 books of dialect poems, *Songs of Jamaica* and *Constab Ballads*. (His regular job was as a policeman in the Kingston constabulary.) These were the first books of poetry written in West Indian dialect to be published in the islands.

Shortly after his books were published, McKay came to the United States. He attended Kansas State University, where for the first time he was exposed to socialism, an ideology he would adhere to for much of his life. Two years later he left for New York City. After an unsuccessful stint as a restaurateur, McKay worked at many of the jobs typically held by West Indian im-

migrants of his time—porter, waiter, barboy, and houseman. He continued to write poetry and, through his contributions to the *Liberator*, became friends with its editor, Max Eastman, and his wife, Crystal. Both were staunch socialists, and both believed in McKay. After the Red Summer of 1919, so named because of the bloody race riots that took place across the country, Eastman published seven poems by McKay, among which was the explosive "Roman Holiday":

A sign announces the presence of the New Negro at the Fourth International Convention of the Negro Peoples of the World, held in Harlem in 1924.

> Black Southern men, like hogs await your doom!
> White wretches hunt and haul you from your huts,
> They squeeze the babies out of your women's wombs,
> They cut your members off, rip out your guts!
> It is a Roman Holiday; and worse:
> It is the mad beast risen from his lair,
> The dead accusing years' eternal curse,
> Reeking of vengeance, in fulfillment here—
> Bravo Democracy! Hail greatest power
> That saved sick Europe in her darkest hour.

Poetry like this made McKay a favorite of the New Negro. He unabashedly attacked racism and promised

Born in Jamaica, Claude McKay became a powerful poet and an outspoken leader of the Harlem Renaissance.

the rise of blacks to their rightful place in the world. Although McKay went to Europe in 1923 and did not return to the United States until 1934, he continued to write extensively about Harlem, publishing *Home to Harlem* in 1928.

Black Pride

Although much of the thought of the Harlem Renaissance was concerned with the position of blacks in American society, some blacks had become convinced that their place was elsewhere. Perhaps the most controversial black voice in America in the years leading up to the Harlem Renaissance and then through the 1920s was that of Marcus Garvey. Born in a small town in Jamaica on August 17, 1887, Garvey moved to the city of Kingston as a young man. He worked as a newspaper printer for a while and then attempted to start a newspaper of his own, *Garvey's Watchman*, dedicated to improving the lot of the black worker. When the paper failed, Garvey traveled to Costa Rica, Panama, Honduras, Colombia, and Venezuela in search of work. In each place he visited, Garvey was dismayed by the condition of black workers. In 1912, Garvey went to London, where he became interested in African studies and read Booker T. Washington's autobiography, *Up from Slavery*.

> I read *Up from Slavery* by Booker T. Washington, and then my doom—if I may so call it—of being a race leader dawned upon me. . . . I asked: "Where is the black man's Government? Where is his King and his kingdom? Where is his President, his country, and his ambassador, his army, his navy, his men of big affairs?" I could not find them, and then I declared, "I will help to make them."

In 1914, Garvey returned to Jamaica and formed the UNIA, an organization devoted to the development of black pride and racial solidarity and the organization of black business enterprises. The most important goal of the UNIA was "to promote the spirit of race pride and love." Garvey began UNIA's work in Jamaica by establishing educational and industrial colleges. On March 23, 1916, he came to New York City for the purpose of gauging black Americans' interest in his organization's plans for liberation and enlightenment.

First and foremost, Garvey sought to instill in the black people of America a feeling of pride in their race and its accomplishments. "I stand before you this afternoon a proud black man, honored to be a black man, who would be nothing in God's creation but a black man," he once thundered to an eager audience. He was both eloquent and extreme on the subject of creating black history. "We must canonize our own saints, create our own martyrs, and elevate to positions of fame and honor black men and women who have made their distinct contributions to our racial history." Finally, he insisted that the black race would recapture its past glory. "Be as proud of your race today as our fathers were in the days of yore. We have a beautiful history, and we shall create another in the future that will astonish the world." Although Garvey is often thought of as an advocate of the black Back to Africa movement, the chief thrust of his program was always attaining equality for blacks in America, which he believed could best be obtained through achieving economic self-sufficiency. Although Garvey spoke often of Africa as black America's spiritual homeland and was an untiring champion of political independence for the nations of Africa, many of his close associates insisted that he never envisioned a large-scale return of black Americans to Africa.

Black people in cities such as Boston, Massachusetts, Washington, D.C., and Chicago, Illinois, flocked to hear Garvey speak. Garvey initially appealed mostly to the black southerners newly arrived in the North and to other West Indian immigrants, for both groups were disillusioned by the racism they found in their new homes. Before long, however, his appeal grew broader. Garvey founded a branch of the UNIA in New York City in 1917, and by 1919 he was making the optimistic claim that the UNIA had more than

Although Marcus Garvey's flamboyant personality made him a favorite of the people, he was not especially popular with the intellectual leaders of the Harlem Renaissance. Years after Garvey's death, Martin Luther King, Jr., described him as "the first man of color in the history of the United States to lead and develop a mass movement."

2 million members and 30 branches around the world. While it is difficult to confirm statistics concerning the UNIA, owing to inefficient bookkeeping and Garvey's own penchant for exaggeration, there is no doubt that it attracted more followers than any black organization had up to that time.

In 1918, Garvey founded the *Negro World*, which Claude McKay called "the best-edited colored weekly in New York." At its peak, the *Negro World* had a circulation of more than 60,000 throughout the United States, Canada, the West Indies, Latin America, Europe, and Africa. The front page of the paper proclaimed it to be "a Newspaper Devoted Solely to the Interests of the Negro Race," and the paper itself was devoted to articles on the glories of black history and the philosophy of Garveyism.

In 1919, Garvey purchased an auditorium in Harlem, renamed it Liberty Hall, and gave nightly speeches to as many as 6,000 listeners at a time. His fame as an eloquent speaker grew, and in the next few years, UNIA branches spread across the United States and Canada, to Philadelphia, Pittsburgh, Cleveland, Detroit, Cincinnati, Chicago, Los Angeles, Montreal, and Toronto. That same year, Garvey was confident enough of his following to launch his most ambitious project, the Black Star Line.

The Black Star Line was intended to be a steamship company operated by and for blacks and linking the black communities of the world in commerce and goodwill. Stock was sold for five dollars a share, so that even poor blacks could become stockholders. The stock circulars proclaimed: "Now is the time for the Negro to invest in the Black Star Line so that in the near future he may exert the same influence upon the world as the white man does today." Within three months Garvey had raised enough money to purchase the first ship, and within a year the line owned a total of three. Blacks from all over the world invested in the Black Star Line and thereby in the hope of economic independence.

In addition to the Black Star Line, Garvey established the Negro Factories Corporation in 1919, protesting that for too long blacks had been consumers and not producers. The ultimate aim of the corporation was to manufacture "every marketable commodity" in factories all over the world. In New York City the corporation operated a chain of grocery stores, two restaurants, a printing plant, a laundry, and a dressmaking shop. During the early 1920s, the UNIA and the corporations associated with it employed more than 1,000 blacks in the United States alone.

The UNIA's successes, however, were tempered by the complete failure of the Black Star Line, Garvey's imprisonment for mail fraud, and his eventual deportation. Because Garvey and his UNIA officers knew

For thousands of blacks, owning a share of the United Negro Improvement Association's Black Star Line meant investing in a better future for blacks around the world.

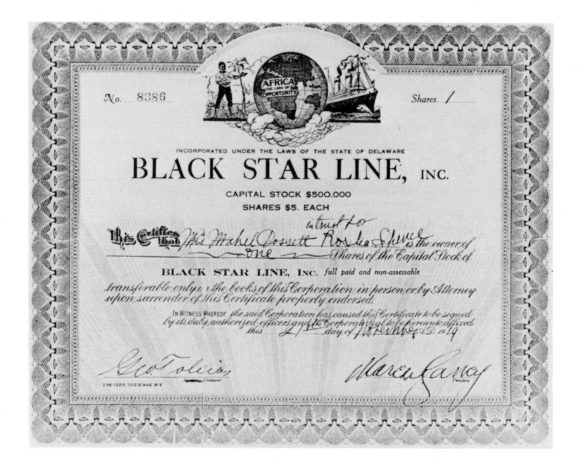

little about running a steamship company and nothing about ships, they were frequently cheated on business transactions. Although the Black Star Line may have been a potent symbol to blacks, it was not a financial success. None of its ships made a single run without economic or mechanical complications. The New York attorney general and the U.S. Federal Bureau of Investigation had been watching Garvey closely for some time, and when rival black leaders accused him of illegalities, government action was swift. Although there was no evidence of anything more than bad management, Garvey was sentenced to five years in prison for mail fraud. He began serving his term in June 1923. Fifty-two months later, President Calvin Coolidge commuted Garvey's sentence, only to have him deported to Jamaica as an undesirable alien. The UNIA movement never regained its popularity.

In many ways, Garvey's philosophy resembled that of the New Negro, yet Garvey was never really accepted by most Harlem intellectuals and was actually hated by many of them. Their differences were largely a matter of personality and public style; for example, Garvey's attacks on other black leaders were delivered in personal, not political, terms. He described the leaders of the NAACP as "near white" and referred to the organization itself as "the National Association for the Advancement of Certain People." Impolitic comments such as these brought particularly vitriolic responses from the black press. Claude McKay, who once had supported Garvey, finally found him too egocentric and intolerant. Du Bois admired Garvey for "tremendous vision, dynamic force, stubborn determination, and an unselfish desire to serve" yet feared that Garvey's "serious defects of temperament and training" made him "the most dangerous enemy of the Negro race."

Nevertheless, Garvey appealed to the masses in a way no other black of his time did. He was not an intellectual but a leader of men; he employed brash or flamboyant tactics that were effective in attracting members but distasteful to those members of the renaissance seeking a more dignified presentation of their cause.

Finally, Garvey was simply more extreme than the Harlem Renaissance intellectuals. Men such as James Weldon Johnson were seeking an equal place for blacks in white society. Claude McKay, who went to the USSR as an American Communist delegate to the Fourth Party Congress, tried to convince its members of the need to specially address the problems of blacks in the United States. His revolutionary vision was still one of whites and blacks working together. Marcus Garvey's vision was different. Garvey dreamed of a world in which blacks could be completely self-sufficient and thus separate from whites. If the white man would not provide opportunities for the black man, the black man would provide them for himself. It was this dream of separation that alienated him from many other black leaders of his time, although Garvey never considered repatriation of blacks to Africa a simple solution to racial problems. Garvey argued that blacks could achieve a desirable degree of separateness and self-reliance within American society through a combination of racial solidarity and capitalistic enterprise.

Ironically, once Garvey was deported, the black press began to admit his influence. "Marcus Garvey made black people proud of their race. In a world where black is despised, he taught them that black is beautiful," read an article in the November 30, 1927, issue of the *New York Amsterdam News*. Garvey continued to work for black enterprises and an African state until he died in 1940, and although he would never again achieve the heights he had in Harlem in the 1920s, this British West Indian left an indelible impression on the consciousness of black Americans.

Sound of Silence

The Great Depression and World War II brought an end to Harlem's era of greatness, and many of the bold ideas that had been so eloquently voiced in the 1920s were not to be heard again until the civil rights and black power movements of the 1960s, when once again, West Indians would help lead the way to freedom.

West Indian emigrants bound for England on board the ship Ascania *in June 1962. Shortly afterward, Britain acted to restrict West Indian immigration and the United States liberalized its immigration policies.*

THE SECOND WAVE

In the 40 years between 1896 and 1936, the population of the British West Indies grew by 50 percent, and in the years after World War II, West Indian immigration began once again to increase. For example, between 1948 and 1954, approximately 20,000 Jamaicans emigrated to the United States, most of them as contract laborers. However, in 1952, the Immigration and Nationality, or McCarran-Walter, Act, greatly reduced West Indian immigration to the United States. Prior to that time, as residents of a British colony, West Indians had qualified for admission under the quota for Britain, which was 65,000 a year. In 1952, new quotas were set for each colonial territory. As a result, only 800 West Indians per year were allowed legal entrance to the United States. However, in 1965, the Hart-Celler Act, whose provisions took effect in 1968, abolished the visa quotas for those islands that had recently become independent or that were shortly to become independent. In doing so, the legislation abolished one of the cornerstones of restrictionist American immigration policy.

Shortly before, Britain's Parliament had acted to restrict West Indian immigration to England. The Hart-Celler Act therefore came as a welcome development to West Indians looking for economic opportunity else-

Federal labor regulations allow for the importation of seasonal agricultural labor from the West Indies. This Jamaican apple picker, at work in Auburn, Maine, in the fall of 1978, was one of 350 Jamaicans brought to Maine that year for the autumn harvest. Since 1943, West Indians, mostly Jamaicans, have also been brought to south Florida to cut sugarcane.

where. By the late 1960s immigrants to the United States from the newly independent countries of Jamaica, Trinidad and Tobago, Guyana, the Bahamas, and Barbados increased enormously. The annual total of all British West Indian immigrants to America rose from about 5,000 in 1962 to more than 25,000 in 1970. By the mid-1970s, the numbers had leveled off to about 20,000 new arrivals per year. Roughly 150,000 British West Indians legally entered the United States from 1962 to 1971; it is thought that thousands more came illegally.

The members of the second wave of British West Indian immigrants are a less homogeneous group than were their counterparts in the first great wave. Most of the earlier immigrants had been members of the British West Indian middle class, professionals and skilled workers. One of the effects of the 1965 Hart-Celler Act was the creation of an opportunity for a greater number of younger, generally less skilled and less educated British West Indians to emigrate to America.

In the early 1960s, the great majority of British West Indians who came to America were well educated and highly trained in their professions. By the late 1960s, the number of unskilled workers had grown, as had the number of unmarried female domestic servants. From 1962 to 1976, the majority of British West Indian immigrants were female. Most British West Indians who came to North America in the 1960s were between the ages of 20 and 49; many were unmarried. Since 1970, there has been a marked increase in the number of West Indian immigrants under the age of 20 and in the number of dependent family members, a development that suggests not only a rise in the immigration of entire families but that the new immigrants intend to make the United States their permanent home.

The New Immigrants

The new immigrants have come to North America to escape the political, economic, and social upheavals that have plagued the West Indies. For example, since the 1970s, Guyana has been experiencing an economic crisis that has left it periodically unable to produce even such staples as flour in quantities sufficient to feed its populace. In 1984, when police raided contraband food traders, they discovered that most of them were housewives hoping to feed their families with small quantities of illegal goods.

The story of Jamaican immigration to North America since the early 1970s is particularly interesting. In 1972, Michael Manley and the People's National party (PNP) were elected to power in Jamaica. Although Manley would not declare the government a democratic socialist state until 1974, working relations between the PNP and the island's private sector soon began to deteriorate. As had happened in the past when changes seemed to threaten the established way of life, the wealthy and the skilled began to emigrate. A yearly exit rate of about 1 percent of the population had already led to the establishment of significant Jamaican communities in London, New York, Miami, and Toronto; 1973 and 1974 saw a marked increase in the immigration to North America of businessmen and officials. Their decision to leave Jamaica was a reaction to a comprehensive political program aimed at instituting egalitarian change in an elitist society. Many whites and those known as the "socially white," that is, upper-class mulattoes, felt threatened by the Manley government's emphasis on African culture and black pride. The rising crime rate and the cry "Is black man time now" further convinced many members of the middle and upper classes to leave the country. In 1976, Jamaica declared a one-year state of emergency

Roy Innis, then director of the Congress of Racial Equality (CORE), speaks to a crowd in Harlem on April 21, 1979. Innis is one of the new generation of West Indian immigrants that has carried on the tradition of political activism established by its earlier counterparts.

A group of African and West Indian Americans enjoy a picnic at Prospect Park in Brooklyn, a borough of New York City that is home to a large number of West Indians.

to deal with a wave of crime and violence associated with the island's economic problems and social unrest. During the emergency, large numbers of businessmen and technical personnel continued to migrate to the United States and to Canada. Increasingly, the middle class in Jamaica felt the lack of economic opportunity and joined their wealthier countrymen in leaving. Since the late 1970s, Jamaicans have accounted for more than a quarter of the West Indian immigrants to the United States.

Because so many of the West Indians who have come to North America in recent years have been relatively uneducated and unskilled, they have made use of new means of obtaining work and a place to live. For example, wealthy Americans often arrange to provide a West Indian woman with a work certificate and a visa by offering her a job as a live-in domestic servant. Others seeking to immigrate may ask a friend or family member already in the United States to open the way to their gaining permanent-residency status by providing them with full-time employment.

Approximately 10,000 British West Indians, mostly Jamaicans, are recruited to work in the sugar fields of Florida each year from fall to spring. This group constitutes the largest single group of foreign workers annually admitted to the United States. At the end of the cutting season, these workers return home to await the next season and the possibility of a job. Although most make more money in America than they can in the West Indies, the work is dangerous, and they are subject to deportation at the whim of the sugar-corporation bosses.

Other West Indians who are not officially sponsored or recruited may choose to enter and reside in the United States illegally. Occasionally, temporary farm workers manage not to return to their native islands and are able to purchase necessary identification documents—a social security card, for example—on the black market. Others ostensibly come to the United States on vacation; once arrived, they "disappear" into off-the-books jobs at garages or restaurants. In order to survive economically, these illegals often hold down several jobs; in order to live undetected by the Immigration and Naturalization Service, they avoid establishing their own residences and live instead with family or friends.

Illegal aliens live in constant fear of deportation, and because their lack of citizenship allows them little legal recourse, many are exploited as cheap labor. A charity worker described their situation to the *New York Amsterdam News:*

Uriel Charles, a Trinidad-Tobagan American, plays a shekere *at a West Indian street festival held in New York City in 1989.*

> We had a Haitian woman who worked as a live-in domestic for a well to do suburban family. She made a meager $80 for 40 hours of work a week. Then there was a Grenadian man who worked 12 hours a day in a funeral home in Brooklyn. They wouldn't give him a half hour lunch break. He would be eating a sandwich with one hand and embalming a body with another.

The presence of illegal aliens has changed the nature and the reputation of many West Indian communities in large urban areas. Once known for their neatness and affluence, some West Indian neighborhoods are becoming run-down. For example, overcrowded housing and schools, garbage pileup, and inadequate hospital care are some of the typical problems confronting the Crown Heights neighborhood of Brooklyn as well as other communities. It is likely that these problems are, to some degree, the result of city governments' inability and unwillingness to account for or provide benefits to a largely undocumented population.

On the East Coast of the United States, benevolent and mutual-aid societies such as the Association of Barbadian Homeowners and Businessmen are no longer the vital organizations they once were. For example, the Grenada Benevolent Association had 500 active members during the 1940s and 1950s. In 1980, a period of greatly increased immigration, only 200 active members were counted. There are several reasons for this representative decline in membership. The absence of official segregation policies in the second half of the century has widened the range of social possibilities open to blacks, lessening the appeal of traditional ethnic clubs, particularly among younger West Indian Americans. Whereas many of the West Indian social clubs and benevolent societies still seek to serve immigrants from one particular island, in recent years West Indian Americans have shown a preference for more comprehensive organizations, such as the National Association of Caribbean American Citizens, a political lobbying group founded in 1979.

The civil rights movement of the 1960s and the growing international movement for black unity and nationalism have led many West Indians in America to identify themselves with the larger black community before the specifically West Indian one. In the 1960s and 1970s, West Indians echoed the powerful black voices of the Harlem Renaissance years and took on new but familiar roles as activists. Roy Innis, born on St. Croix, the Virgin Islands, served as the head of the Congress for Racial Equality (CORE) and as a leader of the early civil rights movement. He helped coordinate the Freedom Summer of 1964, in which bus loads of people, mostly students, rode south to conduct massive voter-registration drives of black citizens. Stokely Carmichael, born in Port of Spain, Trinidad, was another organizer of Freedom Summer, and he later became a leader of the black power movement, which emphasized not only the brotherhood of all blacks but their need to be separate from and independent of whites. Although both Innis and Carmichael were born in the West Indies, Innis, through his work with CORE, chose to identify himself with black Americans, whereas Carmichael, through his adoption of the Pan-African movement, sought a bond with the international black community. (Formulated in the late 19th century, Pan-Africanism asserted that blacks around the world were one people and that Africa was their common homeland.)

Today's Community

The location of the major West Indian communities in America has shifted in the last few decades. According to the 1980 census, 259,037 people in the Northeast identify themselves as West Indian, as do 131,769 in the South, 29,180 in the north-central United States, and 34,928 in the West. There are now sizable West Indian populations in California, New Jersey, and Pennsylvania, but the majority of West Indians still make their home in Miami or in New York City.

In 1979, almost 87 percent of the people entering the United States from independent Caribbean countries claimed New York as their destination. Today, fully one-quarter of New York City's black population is foreign-born, compared with only five percent in 1960. West Indians constitute one of the four largest concentrations of immigrants in New York City, where they live in long-established communities in the Crown Heights, Flatbush, and East Flatbush sections of Brooklyn. That borough is host to the annual West Indian Day Parade and is also home to the Carribean Research Center of Medgar Evers College. In the late 1980s, West Indian communities were established in Queens and the Bronx.

As the West Indian community in New York has grown, it has forged new ties with the native black community. For example, in 1972, 87 percent of the Barbadians living in New York City were married to other Barbadians, but in 1981 an article in the *New York Amsterdam News* reported that most West Indians then living in Brooklyn were married to black southerners. The article speculated that the similar close-knit struc-

Daward Phillips (left), born in Trinidad-Tobago, is an editor of the Daily Challenge, *an African-American newspaper published in New York.*

His Imperial Majesty Haile Selassie, Empress Menen, his wife, the Crown Prince Asfa (center), and Prince Makonnen. Selassie, who ruled Ethiopia from 1930 to 1974, claimed to be a direct descendant of King Solomon.

tures of West Indian and southern black families was one of the factors that made such marriages feasible.

Although it still exhibits some ambivalence concerning American citizenship, the West Indian community in New York City has taken a more aggressive stance in city politics. A Guyanese rector of a West Indian parish in Brooklyn, New York, notes that many of his parishioners "have a strong, romantic association with their homeland"; nevertheless, it is not only the most politically aware West Indians who now make their voices heard in city politics, but the average hardworking West Indian family as well. City politicians recognize the large West Indian community as a vital source of votes, and West Indian festivals have become obligatory stops on their campaign trails. (In 1970, the Caribbean Labor Day parade and celebration in New York City drew more than 1 million people.) Recently, a wave of newly enfranchised West Indian homeowners in the Bronx helped a black candidate oust a state assemblyman of Italian descent. West Indians who have avoided obtaining their citizenship, including those who may have entered the country illegally, seek a more immediate outlet for their ideas and concerns in elections for local school boards and community planning boards, in which one does not have to be a citizen in order to vote.

Although the world of music and dance has greatly changed since slaves brought African musical traditions to America and West Indian immigrants introduced carnival bands and their distinct brand of theater, West Indian music continues to influence American culture in exciting ways. This is most obvious in the recent popularity of reggae, a musical tradition that springs from Rastafarianism.

Rastafarianism has its roots in the Back to Africa movement created by Marcus Garvey. It originated in Jamaica in 1930 when the prince Ras Tafari ("Ras" means "Lord," and Tafari is a family name) was crowned Emperor Haile Selassie I of Ethiopia, King of

The charismatic Bob Marley was instrumental in bringing Rastafarianism and reggae to a worldwide audience.

Born in Jamaica, Annette Burke is the office manager of a New York publishing house. The increased number of young and female immigrants is one way in which the most recent wave of West Indian immigrants differs from earlier generations.

Kings, Lord of Lords, All Conquering Lion of Judah. The central doctrine of Rastafarianism is that Haile Selassie is the god of the black race, a belief that persists in spite of Selassie's having died in 1975. Rastas believe that they are descended from the black Hebrews exiled in Babylon and that they are the true Israelites. Rastafarianism is a millenarian movement, emphasizing the belief that through the power of a supernatural being its members will be delivered from their oppression to a heaven on earth where the glory of the black race will be made manifest.

Although the early Rastafarian movement drew its members largely from the disadvantaged and the unemployed, today it also includes many educated people and some professionals. Its members generally are vegetarians and avoid alcohol. They believe that the hair is part of the spirit, and so it is never combed or cut but worn in "dreadlocks." Marijuana is considered a holy herb and a sacramental gift.

It is estimated that 50,000 Rastas live in Great Britain and that almost 1 million live in the United States. Of this number, approximately 80,000 live in New York City, mainly in Brooklyn. Rastas do not vote in political elections, a fact that must be taken into consideration when determining the nature and extent of the West Indian community's involvement in city politics.

Rastafarianism has had an enormous effect on Jamaican culture, particularly painting, sculpture, and music. Reggae is now one of the most popular forms of Caribbean music in the world. Its distinctive sound—the hypnotic rhythm of drums and guitars, lilting, loping melodies, and the chantlike vocals—has become familiar to millions, many of them non–West Indian. Its best-known performer, and Rastafarianism's most prominent spokesperson, was Bob Marley, who died in 1981.

On the whole, West Indian communities in the United States are thriving. Studies have shown that the mean income of West Indian Americans is several thousand dollars higher than the mean income of American blacks and only a few hundred dollars below

the mean income of American whites. Studies of British West Indian enterprise indicate that they own more than half of the black businesses in New York City and that they are particularly well established in taxi companies, real estate, publishing, advertising, banking, insurance, and retail clothing. Each generation of West Indian Americans has made significant advances. In 1967, for example, 73 percent of second-generation West Indian Americans had graduated from high school, as opposed to 48 percent of first-generation islanders and 43 percent of children of black migrants from the South. Although the comparative lack of education and skills of the new generation of immigrants might lead one to wonder if their advancement will be as rapid, there is every reason to believe that the West Indian–American community will continue to prosper.

President George Bush introduces his nominee for chairman of the Joint Chiefs of Staff, General Colin L. Powell (in uniform) to the press on the West Lawn of the White House in the summer of 1989. The son of Jamaican immigrants, Powell served two tours of duty in Vietnam, where he won a Bronze Star for valor and a Purple Heart.

VOICES OF THE PEOPLE

The West Indian–American community takes justifiable pride in its history of achievement in America. The typical West Indian immigrant overcame obstacles of prejudice and through sheer hard work parlayed whatever advantages of education and training he or she possessed into a better life for his or her family, in the process laying the groundwork for even greater success for his or her children. Still, despite the great success enjoyed by the community at large, there are those whose achievements set them apart, often because their careers have placed them in the public eye and enabled them to speak for their people. Malcolm X, Shirley Chisholm, and Sidney Poitier inherited and built upon the legacy created by James Weldon Johnson, Claude McKay, Marcus Garvey, and others. In the years to come, a new generation of West Indian Americans will no doubt build upon their work.

The Dream of a Black Nation

Malcolm X was born Malcolm Little in 1925. His father, a preacher and a devout follower of Marcus Garvey's, taught the doctrine of black nationalism to his congregation during a time when it was dangerous for a black man to publicly express such views. Malcolm's mother was born in Grenada to a black mother and a white father she never knew. When Malcolm was four, the Little home in Lansing, Michigan, was burned down by the Ku Klux Klan. Two years later, his father was horribly beaten by a gang of white men and left to die under the wheels of a streetcar. With his father dead, it became impossible for his mother to support the family, and Malcolm was placed in a foster home.

At the age of 15, Malcolm moved on his own to a black neighborhood in Boston. There he spent his time in pool halls and learned, as Alex Haley would later relate in *Autobiography of Malcolm X*, that "everything is a hustle." For a time he worked as a shoeshine boy in a white dance club, where he supplied his customers with marijuana, bootlegged liquor, prostitutes, and gambling connections. He was finally arrested after starting a burglary ring and was sentenced to 10 years in prison.

While in prison, Malcolm underwent a dramatic conversion to "The Lost-Found Nation of Islam," also known as the Black Muslims. The Black Muslims had been founded in the 1920s by a man alternately called W. D. Fard, Farad Muhammad, Wali Farad, and F. Muhammad Ali. He taught that mankind was originally black and good but with an evil and weak side that was white. At some point in history, the two halves had split, and the whites were given 6,000 years to rule the world, at the end of which time the blacks would once again reign supreme. In the 1960s, the Black Muslim leader Elijah Muhammad, called the Messenger of Allah, taught that the white race had spiritually, emotionally, and morally destroyed the black race, and he invited blacks to unite in a belief in Allah and to give up the white or Christian God. He advocated the virtues of discipline, abstinence, honor, cleanliness, and self-sufficiency. In accordance with Black Muslim teachings, Malcolm adopted Islamic dietary laws, began to pray, and undertook a course of self-education using the texts of Elijah Muhammad and the books available in the prison library.

Upon his release from prison in 1952, Malcolm went to the Black Muslim headquarters in Chicago, met Elijah Muhammad, and changed his name to Malcolm X. (The X replaced Christian surnames given by slave owners and symbolized the loss of a true name.) He started the successful newspaper *Muhammad Speaks* and spent the next few years touring the country, speaking on black nationalism and the Black Muslim faith and advocating that blacks separate themselves from white society and white oppressors (dubbed "blue-eyed devils"). He was a brilliant speaker whose demands were both articulate and uncompromising.

> Not only do I refuse to integrate with you, white man, but I demand that I be completely separated from you in some state of our own or back home in Africa. Not only is your Christianity a fraud, but your "democracy" a brittle lie.

Malcolm X's militancy and outspokenness caused other leaders of the Black Muslims to dislike him. His prominence as a speaker and leader led to jealousy and resentment within the Nation of Islam, and eventually even Elijah Muhammad turned away from Malcolm, fearing that he planned to usurp his position as the

Although their advocacy of armed resistance provoked fear in white Americans, the Black Panthers also stressed the importance of education and established free breakfast programs for schoolchildren. Here, children in Portland, Oregon, enjoy a meal in 1971. The Panthers also provided free medical and dental care for children in Portland.

Nation's head. When in 1964 Malcolm discovered evidence of an internal conspiracy to have him assassinated, he severed his ties with the Nation of Islam.

Malcolm did not abandon his cause. Trips to Africa and the city of Mecca (the spiritual center of Islam) convinced him of the need for blacks around the world to unite in overthrowing their white oppressors, and he still believed that Islam was the most logical foundation on which to build black unity. In 1964, he formed the Organization of Afro-American Unity (OAAU), which was dedicated to his goals of black nationalism and economic self-sufficiency. At the same time, Malcolm rebuked the Black Muslims for having fallen victim to the same corruption as had white Americans—the desire for money and power at the expense of unity and faith.

On February 21, 1965, Malcolm X was shot and killed as he began to speak at a rally in the Audubon Ballroom in Harlem. Although the Nation of Islam repeatedly denied any complicity in his death, in March 1966 three Black Muslims were convicted of murder. Several years later, one gave sworn testimony that the assassination was indeed an act of Black Muslim vengeance.

Well aware of the anger that his uncompromising message aroused, Malcolm had on more than one occasion expressed doubt that he would live long enough to see the publication of his autobiography, but he was never intimidated by the sense of impending death. In the year before he died, he spoke of his dedication to black nationalism at a meeting of the OAAU: "Our political philosophy will be Black Nationalism. Our economic and social philosophy will be Black Nationalism. Our cultural emphasis will be Black Nationalism."

In the late 1980s, Malcolm's life and work has become the focus of interest on the part of a new generation. His militance, his message of black self-sufficiency, his charismatic presence, and his unwillingness to compromise or sell out have informed much of the New Black Aesthetic, as the recent surge of black cultural and political awareness has been termed by critic Nelson George, and the validity of his proposed solutions to the inequities of American society are being debated anew.

Black Power

Stokely Carmichael was born in Port of Spain, Trinidad, in 1941, but poor economic conditions on the island forced his family to move to Harlem when Stokely was a teenager. The education he had received through the British school system in Trinidad helped him to be accepted to Bronx High School of Science, a high school for gifted students in New York City, where he was the only black student.

While at Bronx Science, Carmichael began working with CORE. After graduating from Howard University in 1960, he and 12 other students started the Student Nonviolent Coordinating Committee (SNCC). The 13 of them traveled to the Deep South and moved in with black families in small, usually impoverished and culturally deprived communities, where they taught the people to read and write, set up health clinics, and registered voters. In so doing they paved the way for the famous Freedom Summer of 1964, when bus loads of students from all across the country came south to

Civil rights leader Stokely Carmichael told Esquire *magazine in 1967 that when he learned that blacks in other parts of the country were treated even worse than were blacks in New York, he "started to burn."*

register black voters long denied their constitutional right to the ballot.

Carmichael achieved his most striking success in Lowndes County, Alabama, where before SNCC started its work, no black had ever voted. Twenty-six hundred blacks registered to vote in 1964—300 more than the number of local white voters. SNCC also helped blacks establish a political party called the Lowndes County Freedom Organization, which adopted a black panther as its symbol.

It was while he was working with SNCC that Carmichael developed the idea of "black power." Alternately referred to as black liberation, there was never a definitive consensus on what either term specifically meant, although in *Black Power: The Politics of Liberation in America*, cowritten with Charles Hamilton, Carmichael declared that black power "rests on a fundamental premise: before a group can enter the open society, it must first close ranks. . . . The ultimate values and

Federal voting examiner H. E. Spencer registers John Hatton of Birmingham, Alabama, in January 1966. Both Stokely Carmichael and Roy Innis participated in voter registration drives in the South during the early days of the civil rights movement.

goals are not domination, or exploitation of other groups, but rather an effective share in the total power of the society." When riots broke out at several SNCC-sponsored rallies in Alabama, many whites came to interpret the slogan Black Power as a call to arms. One of the reasons for this association was the nature of the rhetoric used by black militants. Culled from black English, the writings of Malcolm X, and socialist revolutionary literature, the language of black power was often obscene and profane, its purpose to shock the white man out of his complacency.

Eventually, Carmichael became less concerned with the preaching of nonviolent protest and more concerned with the second phase of the civil rights movement, known as the black nationalist phase. In this phase, militancy in both language and action took precedence over the earlier, peaceful tactics advocated by Martin Luther King, Jr., although most of the plans for massive urban guerrilla warfare from the ghettos never advanced beyond the planning stages. Carmichael gave up the presidency of SNCC and began to speak at rallies and on college campuses across America, arguing that only through militant, direct action could the oppressed make themselves free. He advised blacks against fighting in the Vietnam War for the "freedom" of the Vietnamese when they themselves in the United States were still figuratively in chains.

In October 1966 a group of young blacks in Oakland, California, led by Huey Newton and Bobby Seale, organized themselves under the name "The Black Panthers," using the symbol Carmichael had chosen in Lowndes County. The most immediate reason for the group's founding was to patrol the ghettos of Oakland, monitoring the movements of the police, whom Newton and Seale felt were not providing the residents with adequate protection. Although the Panthers claimed that this decision was taken in order to help promote mutual tolerance between the police and the blacks, their decision to be "unified around the gun" inevitably led to violence. The Black Panthers, who referred to themselves as "the children of Malcolm," also proposed a radical 10-point program that called for reparations for past abuses of blacks, the release of all black prisoners, and trials of blacks by all-black juries. When Carmichael spoke in California in 1967, the Black Panthers offered him their services as bodyguards; later that spring, he became their "prime minister." Under his leadership, the Black Panthers became an even more militant organization, engaging in frequent gun battles with the police; in New York City, several of its members were arrested for organizing bomb plots and for public harassment. In spite of these episodes of violence, the Black Panthers claimed to advocate the abolition of war and oppression. They stressed education as a means of developing self-reliance, helped to establish antidrug and health clinics, and organized breakfast programs in 44 cities.

In 1969, Carmichael resigned from the Black Panthers in protest against its spokesman Eldridge Cleaver's view that constructive coalitions could and should be formed with radical white groups. Later that year he moved to Guinea, changed his name to Kwame Touré, and began work for the Pan-African movement. Carmichael defined the Pan-African ideology as an increased awareness and acceptance by American blacks of the culture, heritage, and ideas of the Africans. For Carmichael, Pan-Africanism has become the ultimate expression of black power. For almost 20 years he has traveled the world lecturing in favor of both socialism and Back to Africa nationalism, but he will always be best remembered as the man who gave voice to the black power movement in America.

The Voice of Black Women

Shirley Chisholm was born Shirley St. Hill in Brooklyn in 1924. When the depression left her parents unable to afford to raise their children in the United States, she and her sisters were sent to live with relatives in Barbados. When she returned to the United States at age 11, the superior Barbadian education she had received allowed her to skip 2 grades. She graduated from Brooklyn College in 1946, then taught at a nursery school while working toward an M.A. in education (which she received in 1952) at Columbia University.

An exultant Shirley Chisholm after learning that she had defeated James Farmer, former head of CORE, in their race for the congressional seat from Bedford-Stuyvesant in Brooklyn. Chisholm's victory on November 5, 1968, made her the first black woman member of Congress.

Chisholm then became the head of the Hamilton-Madison Child Care Center on the Lower East Side of Manhattan, which provided daily care for 150 black and Puerto Rican children. Before long, she became active in local politics. Her Brooklyn neighborhood, Bedford-Stuyvesant, had always been represented in the state government by white men, although most of its residents were black. Many residents felt that these politicians were more concerned with the needs of the party that had paid for their campaigns than with the needs of the community. In response to this indifference, a West Indian named Wesley Holder and several others formed a group called the Bedford-Stuyvesant Political League. The league's first goal was to get a black man elected as judge in the Brooklyn municipal court.

In order to win the election, the league had to convince the members of the black community to vote. Few local residents wanted to have anything to do with the white man's world of politics; most had never even registered to vote. Chisholm began work by organizing a large-scale voter-registration drive. In 1953, the black candidate, Lewis Flagg, was elected as judge.

A harrowing scene from The Defiant Ones, *a 1958 motion picture thriller starring Sidney Poitier and Tony Curtis as a pair of escaped convicts chained together at the wrist.*

Seven years later, Chisholm helped form the Unity Democratic Club. The organization's purpose was to put a black man in the New York State Legislature. They were defeated in 1960, but in 1962, Tom Jones, the club's candidate, was elected to the New York State Assembly. That same year, after having run the Hamilton-Madison Child Care Center for more than 10 years, Chisholm was appointed New York City's chief consultant on day care. When Jones's term ended, Chisholm succeeded him as a candidate and was elected to the state assembly, where she earned a reputation for honesty and hard work. Her most important work was securing the passage of a bill that provided funds and other assistance for college students from poor or minority families.

In 1968, Chisholm became the first black woman to run for a seat in the U.S. House of Representatives. She faced a formidable opponent, James Farmer, a founding member of CORE, but the tenacity that had earned her the nickname "Fighting" Shirley Chisholm served her in good stead. She was fond of saying that "the only thing people in Brooklyn are afraid of in Shirley Chisholm is her mouth," and to remind people of her honesty and independence, she chose the campaign slogan Unbought and Unbossed. In 1969, Shirley Chisholm became the first black woman to be sworn into the U.S. Congress.

Although frustrated by the seniority system in the House, which reserved important committee assignments for senior members, Chisholm was an articulate and well-respected advocate of increased spending for education and social programs during her two terms in Congress. So much so that in 1972, Chisholm became the first black woman to run for president of the United States. Although she lost the campaign, Chisholm's example served to show women and blacks that the government was not the exclusive province of white men and that it was important for America's minorities to be heard.

The Voice of Black Men

Like no other black actor, Sidney Poitier opened the worlds of theater and film to an entire race of artists. Throughout his career as actor and director, he has always attempted to portray an image of the black man that would "make Negroes in the theatre sit up tall."

Poitier was born in Miami, but his family moved to Cat Island, a tiny island in the Bahamas, when he was young; they returned to the United States when Poitier was 15. Like so many West Indian immigrants, he was shocked by the racial prejudice he encountered in America. Hearing that racial tensions were less aggravated in New York City, he moved north, but life there was not all that much better than it had been in the South. After a year of unhappiness, Poitier joined the army. Unfortunately, the military life did not suit him either, and upon leaving the service, Poitier still had no idea of what he wanted to do.

While looking through the help-wanted ads of a newspaper, Poitier spotted an advertisement for actors placed by the American Negro Theater and decided to audition, but because he was a slow reader and had a nearly unintelligible West Indian accent, he was told to "go find a job as a dishwasher." Deeply humiliated, Poitier decided to prove to himself and to the theater that he could indeed act. He began to listen carefully to the radio to try to erase his accent. He read the newspaper aloud from cover to cover, stopping to look up each unfamiliar word. After a year, Poitier was able to land bit parts with the American Negro Theater. While acting in an all-black production of the classical Greek comedy *Lysistrata*, he was spotted by a Hollywood director and offered a screen test.

In 1950, Poitier played the lead role in *No Way Out*, a film about a middle-class black doctor threatened by the brother of a white patient who died under his care. Poitier's character arranges to have himself arrested for murder so that an autopsy will be performed on the dead patient. The doctor risks his career but vindicates himself. *No Way Out* was a breakthrough in the American cinema's portrayal of the black man and of racial injustice.

The film was highly controversial and in most states was either banned or censored. As the civil rights movement grew stronger and more vocal, films that directly addressed the issue of racism became more popular. In 1958, Poitier costarred with Tony Curtis in a film called *The Defiant Ones*. Poitier and Curtis played escaped convicts handcuffed to each other. The film's advertisements made obvious the tensions between the two men. Poitier's and Curtis's characters were portrayed face-to-face, crouched like wrestlers, their wrists cuffed together. The men begin their relationship despising each other but during the course of their adventures gain a mutual respect and tolerance.

Five years later, Poitier won an Oscar for his role as the handyman in *Lilies of the Field*. In 1967, he made *In the Heat of the Night*, *To Sir with Love*, and *Guess Who's Coming to Dinner*, all popular successes. Poitier had managed to become a top box office draw without compromising his ideal of portraying strong and proud black men. In the 1970s and 1980s Poitier appeared less frequently on-screen, preferring to devote his energies to producing and directing.

Sidney Poitier's commitment to his art and his race helped to break down the lingering and debilitating image of the black as the "lazy plantation Negro," an image that was created in the 19th century by white performers in the minstrel tradition. Most notable and notorious among these white "imitators" was Thomas "Daddy" Rice; through his performances and those of his followers, America's image of the black man became enormously distorted. In 1828, Rice popularized a nonsense song entitled "Jump Jim Crow"; eventually the phrase "Jim Crow" was used to describe segregation laws. Well into the 20th century, blacks were still suffering the negative effects of this stereotype. It was largely through the efforts of Poitier and his colleagues that black artists came to be acknowledged as more than just song-and-dance men.

Sidney Poitier, Malcolm X, Stokely Carmichael, and Shirley Chisholm all received a fair amount of renown for their efforts to demonstrate the worth of their people. Before them, James Weldon Johnson, Marcus Garvey, and Claude McKay received similar acclaim. Yet the lives of hundreds of thousands of other West Indian immigrants and their descendants, anonymous perhaps except to family and friends, are no less important. The immigrant who left the West Indies in search of greater opportunity, who overcame the barriers of racism and poverty, who worked his way up from a porter's position to ownership of a small business and then saw to it that his children attended college, is as representative of the West Indian–American experience as are more celebrated individuals. Collectively, it is the lives of hundreds of thousands of immigrants like these that make the West Indian–American story such an inspiring one.

A young member of the West Indian–American community plays a steel drum at a street festival in New York City. With more West Indians immigrating as families than ever before, the community is likely to remain vibrant and strong.

FURTHER READING

Cooper, Wayne F. *Claude McKay: Rebel Sojourner in the Harlem Renaissance.* Baton Rouge: Lousiana State University Press, 1987.

Cronon, E. David. *Black Moses: The Story of Marcus Garvey.* Madison: University of Wisconsin Press, 1955.

Dunn, Richard S. *Sugar and Slaves: The Rise of the Plantation Class in the English West Indies, 1624–1713.* Chapel Hill: University of North Carolina Press, 1972.

Fleming, Robert E. *James Weldon Johnson.* Boston: Twayne, 1987.

Haley, Alex. *Autobiography of Malcolm X.* New York: Ballantine Books, 1989.

Henry, Paget, and Carl Stone, eds. *The Newer Caribbean—Decolonialization, Democracy, and Development.* Philadelphia: Institute for the Study of Human Issues, 1983.

Johnson, James Weldon. *Autobiography of an Ex-Colored Man.* New York: Knopf, 1927.

Lawler, Mary. *Marcus Garvey: Black Nationalist Leader.* New York: Chelsea House Publishers, 1988.

Parry, J. H., and Sherlock, P. M. *A Short History of the West Indies.* New York: St. Martin's Press, 1966.

Reid, Ira. *The Negro Immigrant.* New York: AMS Press, 1968.

Rummel, Jack. *Malcolm X: Militant Black Leader.* New York: Chelsea House Publishers, 1989.

Winks, Robin W. *The Blacks in Canada—A History.* Montreal and New Haven: McGill-Queen's University Press and Yale University Press, 1972.

INDEX

PICTURE CREDITS

MIRIAM KLEVAN is a free-lance writer who resides in Washington, D.C. She is a graduate of Columbia College.

DANIEL PATRICK MOYNIHAN is the senior United States senator from New York. He is also the only person in American history to serve in the cabinets or subcabinets of four successive presidents— Kennedy, Johnson, Nixon, and Ford. Formerly a professor of government at Harvard University, he has written and edited many books, including *Beyond the Melting Pot, Ethnicity: Theory and Experience* (both with Nathan Glazer), *Loyalties,* and *Family and Nation.*